D0121548

30130 162392863

MARY BERRY'S
Supper for friends

MARY BERRY'S
Supper for friends

Impressive, easy-to-prepare dishes for informal entertaining

DK

LONDON, NEW YORK, MELBOURNE,
MUNICH AND DELHI

Editor ANDREW ROFF
Designer KATHRYN WILDING
Managing editor DAWN HENDERSON
Managing art editor CHRISTINE KEILTY
Senior jacket creative NICOLA POWLING
Senior production editor JENNY WOODCOCK
Production controller BETHAN BLASE
Art director PETER LUFF
Publisher MARY-CLARE JERRAM

Photography EDWARD ALLWRIGHT AND WILLIAM REAVELL

DORLING KINDERSLEY (INDIA)
Editor SALONI TALWAR
Designer NEHA AHUJA
Art Director SHEFALI UPADHYAY
DTP designer TARUN SHARMA
DTP co-ordinator BALWANT SINGH
Head of publishing APARNA SHARMA

Material first published in *Mary Berry's Complete Cookbook* in 1995
This edition published in Great Britain in 2009
by Dorling Kindersley Limited
80 Strand, London, WC2R 0RL

A Penguin Company

2 4 6 8 10 9 7 5 3 1

Copyright © 1995, 2007 Dorling Kindersley Limited, London
Text copyright © Dorling Kindersley Limited and Mary Berry

All rights reserved. No part of this publication may be reproduced,
stored in a retrieval system, or transmitted in any form
or by any means, electronic, mechanical, photocopying, recording
or otherwise, wiithout the prior written permission
of the copyright owner.

A CIP catalogue record for this books is available
from the British Library.

ISBN 978-1-4053-4018-2

Printed in
China by Leo

See our complete catalogue at
www.dk.com

CONTENTS

**Essex County
Council Libraries**

INTRODUCTION

Cooking for friends is what I love most about food. Dinner parties give you the chance to catch up with family and friends, so it's great to spend more time chatting and less time cooking. In this book, I've put together a collection of my favourite recipes that are easy to prepare, guaranteed to impress, and taste great.

Hosting a supper party needn't be stressful. Each of the recipes I've chosen are easy to follow and fuss free. Step-by-step instructions and a beautiful photograph of the finished dish ensure success.

Most guests enjoy a relaxed and simple supper, whether you're in the dining room or around the kitchen table. Risottos and stir-fries are simple, tasty dishes that can provide however many portions you need. Prepare one-pot dishes, such as Boston Baked Beans and Pheasant Stew, ahead, leave them to cook on the stove, and serve up when you're ready. Salads and pastas are quick to prepare so you can make a great light meal in minutes. Whatever you're making, try to keep everything simple and have fun.

To begin with, I've suggested some menus, which match together complementary starters, main courses, and desserts. These are just a few ideas – be creative with your dish combinations but remember to keep the meal balanced and not too heavy. Try to plan your time efficiently; if you choose an adventurous main course, go for a simple dessert.

When it comes to starters, light food that's packed with flavour is the key. In this chapter, I've chosen various moreish finger foods for nibbling with a glass of wine –

such as Prawn Blini and Cheese Aigrettes – fresh and tasty soups – such as simple French Pea Soup or Bouillabaisse if you're feeling more ambitious – and light plated starters – including succulent Jumbo Prawns with Aioli and fluffy Goat's Cheese Soufflés.

I've split up the main courses section into dishes that will suit your guests' tastes so you can easily choose something suitable. Try Mussel Gratin to impress your friends with an attractive shellfish dish that they can help themselves to. Poultry and Game dishes include such classics as Mustard Chicken and more extravagant delights such as Mushroom-stuffed Quail. Choose a traditional meat dish – Châteaubriand with Béarnaise Sauce is a sure-fire hit – or tempt your guests with something more exotic such as Teriyaki Beef. There is a selection of vegetarian recipes too – your non meat-eating guests will be thrilled that they have something delicious to eat too! Don't worry if you are hosting guests at short notice – make a pasta dish such as Kedgeree or Paella, both simple to make, will cook while you serve your starter and, above all, taste great.

Desserts have the potential to really wow your guests. Fruit desserts are fresh and light and look the part. Rich desserts, such as Hot Chocolate Soufflés and Chocolate Chip Cheesecake, are melt-in-the-mouth classics.

I love to enjoy good food with great company. I hope that, with these recipes, you will too, and you'll invite friends over for plenty more suppers to come.

MENU PLANNERS

These menus provide a light, well balanced meal. They are reliable options to get you started, but be creative – use your own favourite dishes to create your perfect menu.

SUMMER MENU

Summer melon page 62
Salmon with spinach page 80
Side suggestion: Swiss rosti page 214
Mango and lime mousse page 222

WINTER MENU

Three fish terrine page 70
Pheasant stew page 120
Side suggestion: Pommes anna page 206
Hot chocolate soufflés page 240

PREPARE AHEAD

Sardine pate page 58
Marinated chicken with peppers page 122
Side suggestion: Couscous salad page 208
Quick vanilla ice cream page 246

COURSES FOR A CROWD

Hummus page 18
Kedgeree page 178
Side suggestion: French-style peas page 202
Plum crumble page 234

clockwise from top left:
Winter Menu: Three fish terrine, Pheasant stew, Pommes anna, and Hot chocolate soufflés.

MENU PLANNERS

QUICK
Jumbo prawns with aïoli page 56
Duck breasts with raspberry sauce page 106
Side suggestion: Italian fennel page 210
Scotch mist page 238

DECADENT
Goat's cheese soufflés page 66
Châteaubriand with béarnaise sauce page 128
Side suggestion: Creamed spinach page 200
French almond and apricot tart page 228

HEALTHY
Watercress soup page 40
Mustard chicken page 100
Side suggestion: Golden roasted pumpkin page 204
Winter fruit salad page 230

VEGETARIAN
Avocado with tomatoes and mint page 64
Red bean and tomato curry page 160
Side suggestion: Tricolore salad page 198
Floating islands page 242

clockwise from top left:
*Decadent Menu:
Goat's cheese soufflés,
Châteaubriand with
béarnaise sauce, Creamed
spinach, and French almond
and apricot tart.*

Starters

Finger Food

HUMMUS

SERVES 6

2 × 400g (13oz) cans chick peas, drained
2–3 garlic cloves, coarsely chopped
1 tbsp tahini paste, or to taste
3 tbsp olive oil, or to taste
juice of 1 lemon, or to taste
salt and black pepper

TO GARNISH (OPTIONAL)

6 rosemary sprigs
1 red pepper, halved, seeded,
 and cut into strips
12 small black olives

1 Purée the chick peas, garlic, tahini paste, oil, and lemon juice in a food processor or blender until smooth.

2 Add salt and pepper to taste, and more oil, tahini, and lemon juice if desired, then purée again.

3 Spoon into dishes and level the surface. If you like, garnish with rosemary, red pepper, and olives. Serve with melba toast.

Cook's know-how

There are no hard-and-fast rules about the amounts of oil, tahini paste, and lemon juice when making hummus. The best method is to purée the amount suggested, then taste it and see before adding more. Serve chilled if you like.

MAKES 8 PURSES

500g (1lb) tail end of salmon, boned, skinned, and cut into bite-sized pieces
250g (8oz) cooked peeled prawns
lemon juice for sprinkling
250g (8oz) packet filo pastry
60g (2oz) butter, melted
butter for greasing
salt and black pepper
lemon slices and dill sprigs to garnish

WHITE WINE SAUCE

100ml (3½fl oz) dry white wine
300ml (½ pint) double cream
1 tsp chopped fresh dill

MAKING A FILO PURSE

Place one-eighth of the salmon and prawn mixture in the middle of one buttered filo pastry square. Fold 2 sides of filo pastry over the mixture to form a rectangle. Take the 2 open ends and fold one over the filling and the other underneath. Place this parcel on the second buttered pastry square and draw up the edges. Squeeze the pastry together at the neck to seal the purse.

SALMON AND PRAWN FILO PURSES

1 Combine the salmon pieces and prawns. Sprinkle with lemon juice and add salt and pepper to taste. Set aside.

2 Cut the filo into sixteen 18cm (7in) squares. Brush 2 squares with the melted butter, covering the remaining squares with a damp tea towel. Make a filo purse (see left). Repeat to make 8 purses.

3 Butter a baking tray. Add the filo purses, lightly brush with the remaining melted butter, and bake in a preheated oven at 190°C (375°F, Gas 5) for 15–20 minutes, until crisp and golden.

4 Meanwhile, make the sauce: pour the wine into a saucepan and boil rapidly until it has reduced to about 3 tbsp. Add the cream and simmer until it reaches a light coating consistency. Remove from the heat and add the dill and salt and pepper to taste.

5 Pour the sauce into a bowl and garnish with a dill sprig. Garnish the purses with the lemon slices and dill sprigs and serve with the warm sauce.

Healthy option

You can use about 2 tbsp olive oil to brush the filo rather than melted butter, and serve the purses with lemon halves for squeezing rather than the creamy sauce.

CHEESE AIGRETTES

SERVES 10–12

300ml (¹/₂ pint) water
60g (2oz) butter
125g (4oz) self-raising flour
2 egg yolks
2 eggs
125g (4oz) mature Cheddar
  cheese, grated
salt and black pepper
vegetable oil for deep-frying

1 Put the water and butter into a saucepan and bring to a boil. Remove from the heat, and add the flour. Beat well until the mixture is smooth and glossy and leaves the side of the pan clean. Leave to cool slightly.

2 In a bowl, lightly mix the yolks and eggs, then beat into the flour mixture a little at a time. Stir in the cheese. Add salt and pepper to taste.

3 Heat the oil to 190°C (375°F). Lower the mixture a teaspoonful at a time into the oil, and cook very gently until golden brown. Lift out and drain on paper towels. Serve warm.

Cook's know-how

These little deep-fried French savouries made from choux pastry are traditionally cheese-flavoured, but chopped anchovies are sometimes added for extra piquancy.

CANAPÉS

SERVES 4

4 slices of white bread, crusts removed

ANCHOVY TOPPING

1 tbsp mayonnaise
1 or 2 spring onion tops
8 anchovy fillets, drained
4 cooked peeled prawns

CHEESE TOPPING

30g (1oz) full-fat soft cheese
2 spring onion tops, very finely sliced
4 capers

SALAMI TOPPING

15g (½oz) butter
2 slices of salami
4 slices of gherkin

ASPARAGUS TOPPING

1 tbsp mayonnaise
6 asparagus tips, cooked and drained
2 slices of radish
a few parsley leaves to garnish

1 Make the canapé bases: toast the white bread lightly on both sides. Leave to cool.

2 Make the anchovy topping: spread 1 piece of toast with mayonnaise and cut into 4 squares. Cut the spring onion tops into 4 pieces, then make vertical cuts to separate each piece into strands. Cut the anchovies in half and arrange in a lattice pattern on each square. Place a prawn on top, and garnish with the spring onions.

3 Make the cheese: spread 1 piece of toast with soft cheese and cut into 4 squares. Arrange the spring onion slices diagonally across the cream cheese. Place a caper on each square.

4 Make the salami topping: butter 1 piece of toast and cut into 4 rounds with a pastry cutter.

5 Cut each slice of salami in half to make 2 half-moon-shaped pieces. Roll each piece to form a point at the straight end so that a cornet shape is made. Put 1 cornet and 1 piece of gherkin on each canapé.

6 Make the asparagus topping: spread 1 piece of toast with mayonnaise and cut into 4 squares. Halve the asparagus tips lengthways. Halve the radish slices and cut away the centres to form 4 crescents. Put 3 halved asparagus tips on each square, arrange the radish on top, and garnish.

SERVES 8

1kg (2lb) lean raw minced beef
1 small onion, grated
2 garlic cloves, crushed
1 egg, beaten
90g (3oz) fresh breadcrumbs
2 tbsp tomato purée
2 tbsp paprika
2 tbsp chopped fresh coriander
salt and black pepper
3 tbsp olive oil for frying
chopped parsley to garnish
crudités to serve

SESAME DIP

2 tbsp soy sauce
2 tbsp sesame oil
1 tbsp rice wine or sherry
1 spring onion, thinly sliced
1 tbsp sesame seeds, toasted

SPICY MEATBALLS

1 Make the sesame dip: whisk all the ingredients together and set aside.

2 Combine the meatball ingredients in a bowl. Using your hands, roll the mixture into little balls.

3 Heat the oil in a frying pan, and cook the meatballs, in batches, over a medium heat for 5 minutes or until browned, firm, and cooked through. Garnish with the parsley, and serve warm with the sesame dip and crudités.

CHEESE AND OLIVE BITES

SERVES 4

175g (6oz) mature Cheddar
  cheese, grated
90g (3oz) plain flour
15g ($^1/_2$oz) butter, plus
  extra for greasing
1 tsp paprika
$^1/_2$ tsp mustard powder
20 pimiento-stuffed green olives
cayenne pepper and parsley
  sprigs to garnish

1 Work the cheese, flour, butter, paprika, and mustard powder in a food processor until the mixture resembles fine breadcrumbs. Add 1 tbsp water to the mixture and process briefly.

2 Flatten the dough mixture, and wrap around the olives: take a thumb-sized piece of the dough mixture and flatten on a work surface. Place an olive in the middle of the dough. Wrap the dough around the olive, pressing to make it stick. If the pastry is too crumbly and will not stick, add a little water. Repeat with the remaining dough and olives.

3 Butter a baking tray. Add the wrapped olives and bake in a preheated oven at 200°C (400°F, Gas 6) for 15 minutes until the pastry is golden.

4 Remove the cheese and olive bites from the baking tray and leave to cool slightly.

5 Serve warm or cold, sprinkled with cayenne pepper and garnished with parsley sprigs.

PRAWN BLINI

SERVES 6–8

125g (4oz) plain flour
125g (4oz) buckwheat flour
$^1/_2$ tsp salt
$^1/_2$ tsp fast-action dried yeast
450ml ($^3/_4$ pint) milk, warmed
1 egg, separated
sunflower oil for frying

TO SERVE

2 × 75g (2$^1/_2$oz) jars lumpfish roe
   (1 red, 1 black)
125g (4oz) cooked peeled prawns
125ml (4fl oz) crème fraîche
lemon segments and fresh
   chives to garnish

1 Put both types of flour into a large bowl. Add the salt and yeast, then stir together until evenly mixed.

2 Gradually beat in the warm milk to make a smooth batter. Cover the bowl and leave in a warm place for about 40 minutes until the mixture is frothy and has doubled in volume.

3 Beat the egg yolk into the flour and yeast mixture. Put the egg white into a clean bowl and whisk until stiff but not dry, then fold into the mixture.

4 Heat a large non-stick frying pan or griddle, brush with oil, and heat until the oil is hot. Spoon about 2 tbsp batter into the pan for each blini (you should be able to cook 3 or 4 at a time), and cover a moderate heat for 2–3 minutes, or until bubbles rise to the surface and burst.

5 Turn the blini over with a palette knife and cook for a further 2–3 minutes until golden on the other side. Wrap the cooked blini in a tea towel and keep them warm.

6 Cook the remaining batter in batches until all the batter is used up, lightly oiling the pan between each batch.

7 To serve, arrange the blini on warmed plates, with spoonfuls of red and black lumpfish roe, prawns, and crème fraîche. Garnish with lemon segments and chives.

SERVES 4

TARAMASALATA

500g (1lb) smoked cod's roe, skinned
and coarsely chopped
4 small slices of white bread, crusts
removed
4 tbsp lemon juice
1 large garlic clove, coarsely chopped
250ml (8fl oz) olive oil
salt and black pepper

POOR MAN'S CAVIAR

750g (1½lb) aubergines
salt and black pepper
2 shallots, halved
1–2 garlic cloves
4 tbsp lemon juice
4 tbsp olive oil
4 tbsp chopped parsley
2 tbsp tahini paste

SAVOURY DIPS WITH CRUDITÉS

1 To make the Taramasalata: purée the cod's roe in a food processor or blender until smooth. Break the bread into a bowl, add the lemon juice, and let the bread soak for 1 minute. Add to the cod's roe with the garlic, and purée until smooth.

2 Pour the oil into the mixture, a little at a time, and purée until all the oil has been absorbed. Add salt and pepper to taste. Turn the taramasalata into a bowl. Cover and chill for at least 1 hour before serving.

3 To make the Poor Man's Caviar: cut the aubergines in half lengthways. Score the flesh in a lettice pattern, sprinkle with salt, and leave to stand for 30 minutes. Rinse the aubergine halves with cold water, and pat dry with paper towels. Place on a baking tray and bake in a preheated oven at 200°C (400°F, Gas 6) for 20 minutes.

4 Add the shallots and garlic to the baking tray, and bake for 15 minutes. Purée the aubergines, shallots, and garlic with lemon juice, oil, parsley, tahini paste, and salt and pepper to taste in a food processor or until smooth.

5 Turn the dip into a bowl. Cover and chill for at least 1 hour before serving.

6 Serve both dips with crudités and some good quality bread.

Soups

ASPARAGUS SOUP

SERVES 6

250g (8oz) potatoes, chopped
1.5 litres (2¹/₂ pints) vegetable
  or chicken stock
500g (1lb) asparagus
2 garlic cloves, crushed
2 tbsp chopped fresh basil (optional)
salt and black pepper
30g (1oz) butter (optional)

1 Put the potatoes into a large saucepan, add the stock, and bring to a boil. Cover and simmer for 15 minutes or until the potatoes are nearly tender.

2 Meanwhile, cut any woody ends off the asparagus and discard. Cut off the tips, reserve, and chop the stalks into chunks.

3 Add the asparagus chunks and garlic to the pan with the potatoes and cook for 10 minutes, stirring from time to time, until the asparagus chunks are tender. Cook 9 of the reserved asparagus tips for 4 minutes in boiling salted water, and reserve for the garnish.

4 Purée the soup in a food processor or blender until smooth. Return the soup to the rinsed-out pan and reheat. Add the basil, if using, and salt and pepper to taste. Slice the reserved asparagus tips lengthways in half. Serve the soup hot, garnished with the asparagus tips and small nuggets of butter, if wished.

Healthy option

This is a soup for a special occasion and the butter garnish makes it an absolute classic – melted butter is traditional with asparagus. If you are concerned about the fat content, you can garnish with torn basil instead.

ALL SEASONS TOMATO SOUP

SERVES 6–8

30g (1oz) butter
2 onions, coarsely chopped
1 garlic clove, crushed
1 tbsp plain flour
1.25 litres (2 pints) vegetable
  or chicken stock
2 × 400g (13oz) cans tomatoes
1 bay leaf
salt and black pepper
4 tbsp ready made pesto
single cream (optional) and
  fresh basil leaves to garnish

1 Melt the butter in a large saucepan, add the onions and garlic, and cook gently, stirring from time to time, for a few minutes until soft but not coloured.

2 Add the flour to the pan and cook, stirring constantly, for 1 minute.

3 Pour in the stock, then add the tomatoes and their juice and the bay leaf. Season with salt and pepper. Bring to a boil, cover the pan, and simmer gently for 20 minutes.

4 Remove the bay leaf and discard. Purée the soup in a food processor or blender until smooth.

5 Return the soup to the rinsed-out pan, add the pesto, and heat through. Taste for seasoning.

6 Serve at once, garnished with cream (if you like) and fresh basil leaves.

Healthy option

For a really healthy version of this soup, omit the butter, flour, and pesto and simply simmer the onions and garlic with the stock, tomatoes, and bay leaf. Cook for 30–40 minutes to develop the flavours before puréeing, then serve topped with torn basil.

WATERCRESS SOUP

SERVES 6

30g (1oz) butter
1 onion, finely chopped
2 potatoes, coarsely chopped
125g (4oz) watercress, tough
 stalks removed
900ml (1½ pints) vegetable
 or chicken stock
300ml (½ pint) milk
1 bay leaf
salt and black pepper
single cream to garnish (optional)

1 Melt the butter in a large saucepan, add the onion, and cook gently, stirring from time to time, for a few minutes until soft but not coloured.

2 Add the potatoes and the watercress to the saucepan and cook for about 5 minutes until the watercress is wilted.

3 Pour in the chicken or vegetable stock and milk, add the bay leaf, and season with salt and pepper.

4 Bring the mixture to a boil, cover, and simmer very gently for 15 minutes or until the potatoes are tender.

5 Remove the bay leaf and discard. Purée the soup in a food processor or blender until smooth. Return the soup to the rinsed-out pan, reheat, then taste for seasoning.

6 Serve hot, garnishing each bowl with a little single cream if you like.

Cook's know-how

Watercress soup is delicious served chilled in summer. After puréeing, pour the soup into a large bowl, then cover, cool, and chill for at least 3 hours. Taste for seasoning before serving because chilling dulls the flavour slightly. You can also freeze this soup for up to 3 months.

MINTED PEA SOUP

SERVES 4–6

30g (1oz) butter
1 large onion, coarsely chopped
1 tbsp plain flour
500g (1lb) frozen peas
1.25 litres (2 pints) vegetable
  or chicken stock
½ tsp caster sugar
2 large mint sprigs
salt and black pepper
shredded fresh mint to garnish

1 Melt the butter in a large saucepan, add the chopped onion, and cook very gently, stirring occasionally, for about 10 minutes until soft but not coloured.

2 Sprinkle in the flour and stir for a further 1–2 minutes, then add the frozen peas, stock, caster sugar, and sprigs of mint.

3 Bring to a boil, cover, and simmer gently, stirring occasionally, for 5 minutes or until the peas are soft. Do not simmer any longer than this or the peas will lose their fresh green colour.

4 Remove the mint sprigs and discard. Purée the soup in a food processor or blender until smooth.

5 Return the soup to the rinsed-out pan, reheat, and add salt and pepper to taste. Serve hot, garnished with shredded fresh mint.

Cook's know-how

Use fresh peas when in season. You will need about 1kg (2lb) peas in their pods to give you 500g (1lb) after shelling, and they will take 20 minutes to cook in step 3.

CLAM CHOWDER

SERVES 4

500g (1lb) fresh clams in their
   shells, cleaned (see below)
250ml (8fl oz) fish or vegetable stock
45g (1½oz) butter
1 onion, chopped
3 unsmoked bacon rashers,
   rinds removed, diced
2 tbsp plain flour
2 potatoes, diced
750ml (1¼ pints) milk
1 bay leaf
salt and black pepper

1 Put the clams into a large saucepan, add the fish or vegetable stock, and bring to a boil. Lower the heat, cover, and cook over a medium heat for 5–8 minutes until the clam shells open.

2 Discard any clams that have not opened. Set aside 12 clams in their shells for garnish and keep warm. Remove the remaining clams from their shells. Discard the shells and strain the cooking juices.

3 Melt the butter in a large pan, add the onion, and cook gently for a few minutes until soft but not coloured. Add the bacon and the flour, and cook, stirring, for 1–2 minutes.

4 Add the potatoes, milk, strained clam juices, and bay leaf to the pan. Bring to a boil, then lower the heat and simmer for 15 minutes. Add the shelled clams, and heat gently for about 5 minutes. Remove the bay leaf and discard.

5 Add salt and pepper to taste. Serve hot, garnished with the reserved clams in their shells.

PREPARING CLAMS AND MUSSELS

To clean the shells of clams and mussels, hold under cold running water and scrub with a small stiff brush. Use a small knife to scape off any barnacles.

Cook's know-how

If fresh clams are not in season or you want to save time, use 1 × 200g (7oz) jar or can clams in brine, drained. Omit steps 1 and 2 and increase the fish stock to 300ml (¼ pint), then heat the clams through in step 4.

BOUILLABAISSE

SERVES 8

2 tbsp olive oil
1 large onion, chopped
1 small fennel bulb, sliced
4 garlic cloves, crushed
1 tbsp chopped parsley
1 bay leaf
1 litre (1¾ pints) water
600ml (1 pint) fish or vegetable stock
500g (1lb) ripe tomatoes, finely chopped
1 tbsp fresh parsley, chopped
a strip of orange zest
¼ tsp fennel seeds (optional)
2–3 potatoes, cut into chunks
500g (1lb) assorted fish, cut into
    bite-sized pieces
500g (1lb) assorted shellfish, shelled
pinch of saffron threads
salt and black pepper

1 Heat the olive oil in a large, heavy saucepan. Add the onion, fennel, garlic, parsley, and bay leaf, and cook, stirring occasionally, for 5 minutes.

2 Add the water, stock, tomatoes, parsley, orange zest, and fennel seeds (if using). Bring to a boil, cover, and simmer for 30 minutes.

3 Add the potatoes to the soup, cover, and simmer for 10 minutes. Do not stir or the potatoes will break up.

4 Add the fish, shellfish, and saffron, and season with salt and pepper. Cover and cook for a few minutes, just until the fish turns opaque.

5 Remove the bay leaf and orange zest and discard. Serve the bouillabaisse with slices of toasted baguette if desired.

Cook's know-how

Ask your fishmonger to recommend a variety of white fish and shellfish. Ideally, you should have a combination of pieces of chunky white fish with small whole fish, plus two or three different shellfish such as clams, mussels, and prawns.

CUCUMBER AND MINT CHILLED SOUP

SERVES 4–6

600g (1lb 3oz) plain yogurt
250ml (8fl oz) water
1 cucumber, seeded (see below)
   and diced
4 garlic cloves, coarsely chopped
1 tbsp olive oil
1 tsp white wine vinegar
1 tbsp fresh mint, chopped
salt and black pepper
2–3 tbsp chopped fresh mint and
   3 spring onions, thinly sliced,
   to garnish

1 Purée the yogurt, measured water, one-quarter of the diced cucumber, the garlic, oil, vinegar, and mint in a food processor or blender until smooth. Season well with salt and add pepper to taste.

2 Transfer the soup to a large bowl and stir in the remaining cucumber. Cover and chill for at least 1 hour.

3 Taste for seasoning. Sprinkle the soup with chopped fresh mint and spring onions before serving.

SEEDING A CUCUMBER

Trim the cucumber with a small knife, then cut it in half lengthways. With a teaspoon, scoop out and discard the seeds from each cucumber half.

CHICKEN NOODLE SOUP

SERVES 10

1kg (2lb) chicken thighs
500g (1lb) carrots, sliced
½ head celery, chopped
1 small onion, peeled but left whole
2–3 garlic cloves, coarsely chopped
a few parsley sprigs
3 litres (5 pints) water
2–3 chicken stock cubes
salt and black pepper
125g (4oz) thin noodles
chopped fresh dill to garnish

1 Put the chicken pieces into a large saucepan with the carrots, celery, onion, garlic, and parsley. Pour in the measured water and bring to a boil. Using a slotted spoon, skim off the foam that rises to the top of the pan.

2 Lower the heat, crumble in the stock cubes, and season with salt and pepper. Cover and simmer gently for 1 hour.

3 Skim any fat from the surface of the soup. With a slotted spoon, lift out the parsley, onion, and chicken. Discard the parsley. Chop the onion, and shred the chicken meat, discarding the skin and bones. Set aside.

4 Break the noodles into 5cm (2in) pieces and drop them into the soup. Bring to a boil, cover, and simmer for about 10 minutes or until tender.

5 Return the onion and chicken to the soup, heat through, and taste for seasoning. Serve hot, garnished with dill.

Healthy option

To reduce the fat content of the soup, strip the skin off the chicken thighs before cooking. Chicken meat is low in fat and calories; the fatty part is in the skin and just underneath it.

Plated Starters

SMOKED CHICKEN SALAD WITH WALNUTS

SERVES 6

1 smoked chicken, weighing
   about 1.25kg (2½lb)
100ml (3½fl oz) sunflower oil
2 tbsp walnut oil
75ml (2½fl oz) orange juice
¼ tsp ground coriander
¼ tsp caster sugar
salt and black pepper
375g (12oz) mixed salad leaves
4 oranges, peeled and segmented
60g (2oz) walnut pieces

1 Remove the meat from the chicken carcass, and discard all of the skin and any gristle. Cut the meat into thin, neat slices. Put the chicken into a shallow non-metallic dish.

2 In a small bowl, combine the sunflower and walnut oils, orange juice, ground coriander, and sugar. Season with salt and pepper. Pour the mixture over the chicken slices and toss them gently until evenly coated.

3 Arrange the salad leaves, orange segments, and chicken slices on individual serving plates, scatter the walnut pieces over the top, and serve immediately.

Warm duck or turkey salad

Substitute 375g (12oz) smoked duck or turkey breast for the chicken. Gently heat the poultry slices in the dressing, and add croûtons to the salad if desired.

JUMBO PRAWNS WITH AÏOLI

SERVES 4

2 tbsp olive oil
12 uncooked jumbo prawns
  in their shells
1 tbsp chopped parsley
lemon wedges and flat-leaf parsley
  sprigs to garnish

AÏOLI

2 garlic cloves, coarsely chopped
salt and black pepper
1 egg yolk
1 tsp mustard powder
150ml (¼ pint) olive oil
1 tbsp lemon juice

1 Make the aïoli: in a small bowl, crush the garlic with a pinch of salt until it forms a smooth paste. Add the egg yolk and mustard powder, and beat well. Beat in the oil, drop by drop, whisking constantly until the mixture is thick and smooth, and all the oil has been absorbed. Beat in the lemon juice, and add pepper to taste.

2 Heat the oil in a large frying pan, add the prawns, and toss over a high heat for 3–4 minutes, just until the shells turn bright pink. Remove the prawns from the frying pan and drain on paper towels.

3 To serve, arrange the prawns on warmed plates, sprinkle with chopped parsley, and garnish with lemon wedges and parsley sprigs. Serve with individual bowls of aïoli.

Cook's know-how

Uncooked, or raw, prawns are usually grey in colour – it is only when they are cooked that they turn into the pink prawns we are more familiar with. The golden rule when cooking prawns is never to overcook them, so remove them from the heat as soon as they turn pink. Overcooked prawns are rubbery, chewy, and tasteless.

SARDINE PÂTÉ

SERVES 8

2 × 125g (4oz) cans sardines in oil,
  drained, bones removed
125g (4oz) butter, softened
125g (4oz) low-fat soft cheese
3 tbsp lemon juice
black pepper
lemon twists and parsley sprigs to garnish

1 Purée the sardines, butter, cheese, and lemon juice in a food processor until almost smooth. Add pepper and more lemon juice to taste.

2 Divide the sardine mixture between 8 small ramekins (or put into 1 large bowl) and level the surface. Cover and chill in the refrigerator for at least 30 minutes.

3 Serve chilled, garnished with lemon twists and parsley sprigs.

Healthy note

Sardines are an oily fish, rich in omega-3 fatty acids, which can help to discourage heart disease and blood clots. They also provide vitamin D and, if you eat the bones as you do in this pâté, they are an important source of calcium.

Prawn pâté

Instead of the sardines, use 250g (8oz) cooked and peeled prawns.

GRAVADLAX

SERVES 16

2.25kg (4¹/₂lb) whole fresh salmon,
  boned and cut lengthways in half
  into 2 fillets (ask your fishmonger)
dill sprigs and lemon segments
  to garnish

PICKLING MIXTURE

75g (2¹/₂oz) granulated sugar
4 tbsp coarse sea salt
4 tbsp chopped fresh dill

MUSTARD DILL SAUCE

3 tbsp Dijon mustard
2 tbsp caster sugar
1 tbsp white wine vinegar
1 egg yolk
150ml (¹/₄ pint) sunflower oil
salt and black pepper
2 tbsp chopped fresh dill

1 Make the pickling mixture: put the granulated sugar, sea salt, and chopped fresh dill into a small bowl, season generously with black pepper, and stir well to mix.

2 Sandwich the salmon fillets together: put 1 salmon fillet skin-side down on a board, cover the surface with the pickling mixture, and place the second fillet on top, skin-side up.

3 Wrap the fillets in a double thickness of foil and place in a large dish. Weigh down with kitchen weights or heavy cans, and keep in the refrigerator for 24 hours. Halfway through this time, turn the salmon over.

4 Make the mustard dill sauce: in a medium bowl, whisk together the mustard, sugar, vinegar, and egg yolk, then whisk in the oil a little at a time. The sauce should have the consistency of mayonnaise. Add salt and pepper to taste, and stir in the chopped dill.

5 Unwrap the gravadlax. A lot of sticky, salty liquid will drain from the fish when it has been pickled: this is quite normal. Remove the fish from the pickling liquid, and dry well. Separate the 2 salmon fillets.

6 To serve, slice each fillet on the slant, cutting the flesh away from the skin. The slices should be a little thicker than for smoked salmon and should have a fringe of dill. Garnish with dill sprigs and lemon segments, and serve with the mustard dill sauce.

SUMMER MELONS

SERVES 4

2 × 750g (1½lb) ripe melons with
   different coloured flesh (see box, right)
500g (1lb) tomatoes
1 tbsp chopped fresh mint
mint sprigs to garnish

DRESSING

90ml (3fl oz) sunflower oil
2 tbsp white wine vinegar
¼ tsp caster sugar
salt and black pepper

1 Cut the melons in half, and remove and discard the seeds. Using a melon baller or a knife, cut balls or neat cubes of flesh into a bowl.

2 Peel the tomatoes: cut out the cores and score an "x" on the base of each one, then immerse in a bowl of boiling water until the skins start to split. Transfer at once to a bowl of cold water. Peel and seed the tomatoes, then cut the flesh into long strips. Add the strips to the melon.

3 Make the dressing: in a small bowl, whisk together the sunflower oil and vinegar, then add the caster sugar, and salt and pepper to taste. Pour the dressing over the melon and tomato mixture. Cover and chill for at least 1 hour.

4 To serve, stir the chopped mint into the melon and tomato mixture, spoon the salad into chilled bowls, and garnish each serving with a mint sprig.

Cook's know-how

Choose two or three varieties of melon to make an attractive colour combination. Honeydew has pale greenish yellow flesh, cantaloupe has either pale green or orange flesh, Ogen and Galia have pale yellow or green flesh, while Charentais melons have deep orange flesh.

AVOCADO WITH TOMATOES AND MINT

SERVES 4

4 small firm tomatoes
2 ripe avocados
1 tbsp chopped fresh mint
mint sprigs to garnish

DRESSING

2 tsp white wine vinegar
1 tsp Dijon mustard
2 tbsp olive oil
$1/4$ tsp caster sugar
salt and black pepper

1 Peel the tomatoes (see left). Seed and then coarsely chop the tomato flesh.

2 Make the dressing: in a small bowl, whisk together the vinegar and mustard. Gradually whisk in the oil, then add the caster sugar, and salt and pepper to taste.

3 Halve and stone the avocados. Brush the flesh with a little dressing to prevent discoloration.

4 Combine the tomatoes, chopped mint, and dressing. Pile the tomato mixture into the avocado halves, garnish with mint sprigs, and serve at once.

Healthy note

Avocados are full of heart-healthy nutrients, such as vitamin E, folate, potassium, and monounsaturated fats, but they are also quite high in calories, so it is best not to eat too many of them too often.

PEELING TOMATOES

Cut the cores from the tomatoes and score an "x" on the base. Immerse the tomatoes in boiling water for 8–15 seconds until their skins start to split. Transfer at once to cold water. When the tomatoes are cool enough to handle, peel off the skin with a small knife.

GARLIC AND GOAT'S CHEESE SOUFFLÉS

SERVES 6

6 × 150ML (¼ PINT) SOUFFLÉ DISHES

1 head of garlic
250ml (8fl oz) milk
125ml (4fl oz) water
45g (1½oz) butter, plus extra
  for greasing
45g (1½oz) plain flour
150g (5oz) goat's cheese, diced
6 eggs, separated
salt and black pepper
fresh chives to garnish

1 Separate and peel the garlic cloves. Put the milk, measured water, and all but one of the garlic cloves into a saucepan. Bring to a boil, then simmer for 15–20 minutes until the garlic is tender and the liquid has reduced to 250ml (8fl oz). Leave to cool. Lightly mash the garlic in the milk.

2 Melt the butter in a saucepan, add the flour, and cook, stirring, for 1 minute. Remove from the heat, and gradually blend in the garlic milk.

3 Return to the heat and bring to a boil, stirring constantly, until the mixture thickens. Simmer for 2–3 minutes. Transfer to a large bowl and leave to cool for about 10 minutes. Chop the remaining garlic clove.

4 Add the chopped garlic, diced goat's cheese, and egg yolks to the cooled sauce. Season with salt and pepper.

5 In a large bowl, whisk the egg whites until stiff but not dry. Stir 1 tbsp of the egg whites into the garlic and cheese mixture, then fold in the remaining egg whites.

6 Lightly butter the soufflé dishes, pour in the soufflé mixture, and bake in a preheated oven at 180°C (350°F, Gas 4) for 15–20 minutes. Serve at once, garnished with chives.

BRANDIED CHICKEN LIVER PÂTÉ

SERVES 8

1KG (2LB) LOAF TIN OR TERRINE

125g (4oz) bread, crusts removed
1 garlic clove, coarsely chopped
125g (4oz) streaky bacon rashers,
    rinds removed, coarsely chopped
2 tsp chopped fresh thyme
500g (1lb) chicken livers, trimmed
1 egg
4 tbsp brandy
½ tsp grated nutmeg
salt and black pepper
60g (2oz) butter, melted

1 Line the loaf tin with foil, leaving 5cm (2in) foil overhanging on each side.

2 Cut the bread into thick chunks, and work them with the garlic in a food processor to form fine breadcrumbs. Add the bacon and thyme, and work until finely chopped.

3 Add the chicken livers, egg, brandy, and nutmeg, season with salt and pepper, and purée until smooth. Add the butter and purée again.

4 Put the pâté mixture into the prepared loaf tin, level the surface, and fold the foil over the top. Place in a roasting tin, pour in boiling water to come about halfway up the side of the loaf tin, and bake in a preheated oven at 160°C (325°F, Gas 3) for 1 hour.

5 Test the pâté for doneness: insert a skewer into the middle. If it comes out hot and clean, the pâté is cooked. Leave the pâté to cool completely, then cover, and leave to chill in the refrigerator overnight.

6 To serve, cut the pâté into slices and serve with a simple salad and melba toast.

THREE FISH TERRINE

SERVES 10

1.25 LITRE (2 PINT) LOAF TIN OR TERRINE

sunflower oil for greasing
175–250g (6–8oz) smoked salmon slices
salt and black pepper
watercress to serve

TROUT PÂTÉ

175g (6oz) smoked trout
90g (3oz) butter
90g (3oz) full-fat soft cheese
1½ tbsp lemon juice

SALMON PÂTÉ

125g (4oz) smoked salmon pieces
60g (2oz) butter
60g (2oz) full-fat soft cheese
1½ tbsp lemon juice
1 tbsp tomato purée
1 tbsp chopped fresh dill

MACKEREL PÂTÉ

175g (6oz) smoked mackerel
90g (3oz) butter
90g (3oz) full-fat soft cheese
1½ tbsp lemon juice

1 Make the trout pâté: remove the skin and bones from the trout and purée with the butter, cheese, lemon juice, and salt and pepper to taste in a food processor until smooth and well blended. Turn into a bowl, cover, and chill.

2 Make the salmon pâté: purée the smoked salmon pieces, butter, cheese, lemon juice, tomato purée, dill, and salt and pepper to taste in a food processor until smooth and well blended. Turn into a bowl, cover, and chill.

3 Make the mackerel pâté: remove the skin and bones from the mackerel and purée with the butter, cheese, lemon juice, and salt and pepper to taste in a food processor until smooth and well blended. Turn into a bowl, cover, and chill.

4 Assemble the terrine: oil the loaf tin and line with overlapping slices of smoked salmon. Arrange them crossways and allow 3.5–5cm (1½–2in) to overhang the sides of the tin. Turn the trout pâté into the loaf tin and spread it evenly with a palette knife, levelling the surface. If necessary, wet the knife to prevent sticking. Add the salmon pâté in the same way, and then top with the mackerel pâté. Fold the smoked salmon over the mackerel pâté, tucking in the ends.

5 To serve, carefully turn out the terrine, cut into thick slices, and arrange on beds of watercress on individual serving plates.

Main Courses

Fish and Shellfish

THAI PRAWN STIR-FRY

SERVES 4

250g (8oz) rice noodles
salt
3 tbsp sunflower oil
1 red pepper, halved, seeded,
   and cut into thin strips
1 carrot, cut into thin strips
1 fresh green chilli, halved, seeded,
   and cut into thin strips
2.5cm (1in) piece of fresh root ginger,
   peeled and cut into thin strips
1 garlic clove, crushed
8 spring onions, sliced
2 lemon grass stalks, trimmed and sliced
500g (1lb) cooked peeled tiger prawns
2 tbsp white wine vinegar
2 tbsp soy sauce
juice of ½ lime
1 tbsp sesame oil
3 tbsp chopped fresh coriander
   to garnish

1 Put the rice noodles into a large saucepan of boiling salted water and stir to separate the noodles. Turn off the heat, cover, and leave to stand for 4 minutes. Drain well and set aside.

2 Heat 1 tbsp of the sunflower oil in a wok or large frying pan. Add the red pepper, carrot, chilli, ginger, garlic, spring onions, and lemon grass, and stir-fry over a high heat for 2 minutes.

3 Add the prawns, and stir-fry for 1 minute, then stir in the noodles.

4 Add the remaining sunflower oil, the vinegar, soy sauce, lime juice, and sesame oil, and stir-fry for 1 minute.

5 Sprinkle with the chopped fresh coriander, and serve at once.

Scallop stir-fry

Substitute 500g (1lb) shelled scallops for the tiger prawns, cutting each scallop into two or three pieces if they are large. Stir-fry for about 2 minutes, then add the red pepper, carrot, chilli, fresh root ginger, garlic, spring onions, and lemon grass, and stir- fry for a further 2 minutes. Add the soaked and drained noodles, then continue with the recipe from the beginning of step 4.

SCALLOPS WITH ASPARAGUS AND LEMON

SERVES 6

500g (1lb) fresh asparagus tips, chopped into 2cm (1in) lengths
60g (2oz) butter
500g (1lb) queen scallops
3 garlic cloves, crushed
juice of 1 lemon
2 tbsp finely chopped parsley
1 tbsp chopped fresh tarragon
salt and black pepper
rice with saffron to serve

1 Blanch the asparagus in boling salted water for about 2 minutes, then drain and refresh in cold water to stop the cooking and set the bright green colour.

2 Melt half the butter in a frying pan, and fry the scallops for about 30 seconds on each side until just opaque and firm to the touch (you may need to do this in batches). Remove the scallops with a slotted spoon, and keep warm.

3 Heat the remaining butter in the frying pan. Add the garlic, lemon juice, parsley, and tarragon, and season with salt and pepper.

4 Return the scallops and asparagus to the pan and heat them through very gently, shaking the pan to coat them in the sauce. Serve with saffron rice.

Cook's know-how

If queen scallops are not available, use the larger king scallops instead. Slice each one in half horizontally, and they will then cook in the same amount of time. If scallops are not available at all, or if you prefer, you can substitute an equal quantity of raw tiger prawns. Peel them, but leave the tails on for a decorative touch.

SALMON WITH SPINACH

SERVES 4

4 × 175g (6oz) slices salmon fillets
salt and black pepper
15g (¹/₂oz) butter
lemon wedges to garnish

SPINACH SALSA

2 tbsp olive oil
8 spring onions, finely sliced
1 garlic clove, crushed
4 tbsp lemon juice
1 tsp wholegrain mustard
500g (1lb) spinach,
  finely chopped

1 Season the salmon fillets with black pepper and dot with the butter.

2 Cook the salmon fillets under a hot grill, 7cm (3in) from the heat, for 2–3 minutes on each side until the fish is opaque and the flesh flakes easily. Leave to rest.

3 Make the spinach salsa: heat the oil in a frying pan, add the spring onions and garlic, and cook, stirring, for about 1 minute. Stir in the lemon juice, mustard, and spinach, and cook, stirring, for about 2 minutes. Transfer to a bowl, and season with salt and pepper.

4 Garnish the salmon with lemon wedges and serve at once, with the salsa.

Healthy note

Spinach is not as rich in iron as was previously thought, although it does contain a useful source. One of its main benefits to good health is that it contains a phytochemical called lutein, an antioxidant that can help protect against age-related degeneration of eyesight.

SERVES 4

60g (2oz) plain flour
salt and black pepper
4 small lemon sole, each cut into 4
   fillets and skinned (see box, below)
60g (2oz) butter
1 tbsp chopped parsley
juice of ½ lemon
lemon slices and parsley
   sprigs to garnish
boiled vegetables to serve

FILLETS OF SOLE MEUNIÈRE

1 Sprinkle the flour on to a plate and season with salt and pepper. Dip the 16 fillets into the seasoned flour and shake off any excess.

2 Melt half of the butter over a medium heat in a large frying pan. When it is foaming, add the fillets, and cook for 2 minutes on each side or until the flesh is opaque and flakes easily. Transfer to warmed serving plates and keep warm.

3 Wipe the pan with paper towels. Melt the remaining butter and heat quickly until golden. Stir in the parsley and lemon juice, then pour over the fillets. Serve hot with boiled vegetables and garnished with lemon and parsley.

Cook's know-how

You can fillet and skin the sole yourself, but your fishmonger will do it for free, and this will save a lot of time. Explain that you need "quarter" fillets from each sole, that is two slim fillets from each side of the fish. For a special occasion you can use Dover sole, sometimes described as the king of sole. It is less widely available than lemon sole, and more expensive, but the flavour is superb.

MUSSEL GRATIN

SERVES 4

150ml (¼ pint) dry white wine
1 shallot, finely chopped
1 garlic clove, crushed
3kg (6lb) large mussels,
  cleaned and beards removed
300ml (½ pint) single cream
3 tbsp chopped parsley
salt and black pepper
30g (1oz) fresh white breadcrumbs
30g (1oz) butter, melted

1 Pour the wine into a large saucepan, add the chopped shallot and crushed garlic, and bring to a boil. Simmer for 2 minutes.

2 Add the mussels, cover tightly, and return to a boil. Cook, shaking the pan frequently, for 5–6 minutes until the mussels open.

3 Using a slotted spoon, transfer the mussels to a large bowl. Discard any that have not opened; do not try to force them open.

4 Strain the cooking liquid into a saucepan, bring to a boil, and simmer until reduced to about 3 tbsp. Add the cream and heat through. Stir in half of the parsley, and season with salt and pepper.

5 Remove the top shell of each mussel and discard. Arrange the mussels, in their bottom shells, on a large flameproof serving dish.

6 Spoon the sauce over the mussels, and sprinkle with the breadcrumbs and melted butter. Cook under a hot grill, 10cm (4in) from the heat, for 3–5 minutes. Garnish with the remaining parsley and serve at once.

Cook's know-how

Mussels are often sold by volume: 900ml (1½ pints) is equivalent to 750g (1½ lb), which will yield about 375g (12oz) shelled mussels.

MONKFISH WITH GINGER-ORANGE SAUCE

SERVES 4

1 orange, washed and thinly sliced
1 onion, chopped
1cm (½in) piece of fresh root
  ginger, peeled and grated
500g (1lb) monkfish fillets, skinned
250ml (8fl oz) fish or vegetable stock
grated zest of ½ lime
75ml (2½fl oz) lime juice
salt and cayenne pepper
60g (2oz) unsalted butter,
  chilled and cubed
sugar or honey to taste (optional)
orange and snipped chives
  to garnish
rice and buttered sweetcorn to serve

1 Put the orange slices, onion, and ginger into a pan. Add the monkfish, spring onions, and stock. Bring to a boil, and simmer, without stirring, for 10 minutes or until the fish is firm. With a slotted spoon, transfer the fish to a serving dish. Keep hot.

2 Put a sieve over a bowl, tip in the remaining contents of the pan and press hard with the back of a spoon to extract all the juices.

3 Pour the juices into a small saucepan and boil rapidly, uncovered, for about 12 minutes until the liquid has reduced to about 2 tbsp.

4 Add the lime zest and juice, season with salt and cayenne, and heat gently, stirring, until warm. Remove from the heat. Add the cubes of butter one at a time, whisking between each addition until the butter melts. The sauce will become glossy at the end. Taste, and add a little sugar or honey if you like.

5 Pour the sauce over the fish, garnish, and serve at once with rice and buttered sweetcorn.

BLACK BREAM NIÇOISE

SERVES 4

2 × 560g (1lb 2oz) black bream, cleaned,
  with heads removed
salt and black pepper
3 tbsp olive oil
1 large onion, sliced
1 small fennel bulb, sliced
1 garlic clove, crushed
12 pitted black olives
2 tbsp chopped parsley
juice of 1 lemon

1 Prepare the bream: make 2 deep diagonal cuts in the flesh on both sides of each bream, using a sharp knife. Put salt and pepper into a bowl and combine. Sprinkle on the inside and outside of the bream.

2 Heat 2 tbsp of the oil in a frying pan, add the onion, fennel, and garlic, and cook gently, stirring occasionally, for 5–8 minutes until the vegetables are soft but not coloured.

3 Spoon the vegetables into an ovenproof dish, and place the bream on top. Scatter the olives and parsley over the fish, sprinkle with the lemon juice, and drizzle with the remaining olive oil.

4 Cover the fish loosely with foil, and bake in a preheated oven at 200°C (400°F, Gas 6) for 15 minutes.

5 Remove the foil and bake for 10 minutes or until the fish is cooked.

Healthy note

Slashing fish through the skin deep into the flesh is not just to make it look more attractive. It allows the fish to cook quicker, which helps retain juices and nutrients.

SERVES 4

500g (1lb) monkfish,
  trimmed and skinned
150ml (¼ pint) fish or vegetable stock
1 slice of onion
6 black peppercorns
squeeze of lemon juice
1 bay leaf
mixed salad leaves, such as
  frisée, radicchio, and rocket
2 avocados
lemon juice for brushing
2 large tomatoes, peeled (page 64),
  seeded, and cut into strips
125g (4oz) cooked peeled prawns
90g (3oz) white crabmeat
flat-leaf parsley to garnish

CRÈME FRAÎCHE DRESSING

125ml (4fl oz) crème fraîche
3 tbsp lemon juice
salt and black pepper

SEAFOOD AND AVOCADO SALAD

1 Put the monkfish into a saucepan with the stock, onion, peppercorns, lemon juice, and bay leaf. Bring to a gentle simmer, cover, and poach very gently, turning once, for 10 minutes until opaque throughout and firm.

2 Remove the pan from the heat and leave the fish to cool in the liquid, then lift it out and cut into bite-sized pieces.

3 Make the crème fraîche dressing: put the crème fraîche and lemon juice into a bowl, add salt and pepper to taste, and stir to mix.

4 To serve, arrange the salad leaves on individual plates. Halve, stone, and peel the avocados, and brush with lemon juice. Slice lengthways and arrange in a fan shape on the leaves. Add the strips of tomato, the monkfish, prawns, and crabmeat. Spoon the crème fraîche dressing over the salad, garnish with the parsley, and serve at once.

Healthy option

You can use low-fat crème fraîche for the cold dressing because it holds its shape well. It is only when you heat crème fraîche that it becomes runny and thin.

SERVES 4

8 small whole squid, cleaned
30g (1oz) butter, plus a little
  extra for frying
1 large onion, finely chopped
2 garlic cloves, crushed
60g (2oz) fresh breadcrumbs
1 tbsp chopped fresh dill
1 tbsp chopped parsley
salt and black pepper
lemon slices and chopped parsley
  to garnish
roasted vegetables to serve

MEDITERRANEAN STUFFED SQUID

1 Chop the squid tentacles roughly and set aside.

2 Make the stuffing: melt the butter in a frying pan, add the onion and garlic, cover and sauté over a low heat for about 15–20 minutes until very soft.

3 Add the chopped squid tentacles, breadcrumbs, dill, and parsley to the onion and garlic, and fry over a high heat for 2–3 minutes. Season with salt and pepper, and leave to cool.

4 Fill the squid bodies with the cold stuffing, and secure the tops, by threading a cocktail stick through the top of each stuffed squid to secure the opening.

5 Heat a little butter in a clean frying pan, and fry the stuffed squid for about 4–5 minutes until golden brown all over and firm to the touch, and the filling is heated through.

6 Garnish the squid with the lemon slices and parsley, and serve at once with roasted vegetables.

SERVES 4–6

300ml (½ pint) milk
1 slice of onion
6 black peppercorns
1 bay leaf
60g (2oz) butter, plus extra for greasing
750g (1½lb) haddock fillet, skinned
salt and black pepper
squeeze of lemon juice
250g (8oz) button mushrooms, sliced
30g (1oz) plain flour
3 tbsp single cream (optional)
30g (1oz) fresh white breadcrumbs
30g (1oz) Parmesan cheese, grated
chopped parsley to garnish
carrots to serve

HADDOCK WITH PARMESAN CRUST

1 Put the milk into a small saucepan with the onion, peppercorns, and bay leaf, and bring just to a boil. Remove from the heat, cover, and leave to infuse for 10 minutes. Lightly butter a shallow ovenproof dish.

2 Cut the haddock into 7cm (3in) pieces, and place in a single layer in the dish. Sprinkle with salt and pepper.

3 Melt half of the butter in a saucepan, add the lemon juice and mushrooms, and season with salt and pepper. Cook gently, stirring occasionally, for 3 minutes or until just tender. Remove the mushrooms with a slotted spoon and put them on top of the fish.

4 Strain the infused milk and set aside. Melt the remaining butter in a saucepan, add the flour, and cook, stirring, for 1 minute. Remove from the heat and gradually blend in the infused milk. Bring to a boil, stirring until the mixture thickens. Simmer for 2–3 minutes. Stir in the cream, if using, and season with salt and pepper.

5 Pour the sauce over the fish and mushrooms, then sprinkle with the breadcrumbs and Parmesan. Bake in a preheated oven at 190°C (375°F, Gas 5) for 25–30 minutes until the fish is cooked and the top is golden and bubbling. Garnish with parsley, and serve at once with carrots.

SALMON EN CROÛTE

SERVES 8

1.7–2kg (3¹/₂–4lb) salmon, cleaned
  and filleted, then cut lengthways in
  half and skinned
1 tbsp chopped fresh dill
grated zest and juice of 1 lemon
salt and black pepper
30g (1oz) butter
8 spring onions, sliced
250g (8oz) spinach, coarsely shredded
250g (8oz) low-fat soft cheese
plain flour for dusting
750g (1¹/₂lb) puff pastry
1 egg, beaten
lemon slices, cherry tomatoes,
  and parsley sprigs to garnish

1 Put the 2 pieces of salmon into a shallow non-metallic dish and sprinkle with the dill, lemon zest and juice, and salt and pepper. Cover and leave to marinate in the refrigerator for about 1 hour.

2 Melt the butter in a small pan, add the onions, and cook gently for 2–3 minutes until soft but not coloured. Remove from the heat.

3 Add the spinach, toss in the butter, then leave to cool. Stir in the cheese, and season with salt and pepper.

4 Roll out half of the pastry on a lightly floured surface to a 20 × 38cm (8 × 15in) rectangle. Put the pastry on a baking tray, and place 1 salmon fillet, skinned side down, on top. Spread with the spinach mixture, then put the second salmon fillet on top, skinned side up. Brush the pastry border with a little beaten egg.

5 Roll out the remaining pastry to a slightly larger rectangle, cover the salmon completely, then trim and seal the edges. Make "scales" on the top with the edge of a spoon, then make 2 small holes to let steam escape during baking.

6 Brush with beaten egg and bake in a preheated oven at 200°C (400°F, Gas 6) for 40–45 minutes until the pastry is risen and golden brown. Serve hot, garnished with lemon, tomatoes, and parsley.

Poultry and Game

MUSTARD CHICKEN

SERVES 4

1 tbsp olive oil
4 skinless, boneless chicken breasts, cut
   diagonally into 2.5cm (1in) strips
1 garlic clove, crushed
250ml (8fl oz) single cream
1 tbsp plain flour
1 tbsp coarse-grain mustard
salt and black pepper
flat-leaf parsley sprigs to garnish
basmati rice and wild rice to serve

1 Heat the oil in a frying pan until hot. Add the chicken strips and garlic, in batches if necessary, and cook over a moderate heat, stirring frequently, for 3–4 minutes.

2 With a slotted spoon, lift the chicken and garlic out of the frying pan, and keep them warm.

3 In a small bowl, mix a little of the cream with the flour to make a smooth paste, then mix in the remaining cream.

4 Lower the heat and pour the cream into the pan. Cook gently for 2 minutes, stirring constantly until the sauce has thickened. Stir in the mustard and heat through gently, then season with salt and pepper.

5 Return the chicken to the pan, coat with the sauce, and cook gently for a few minutes more until the chicken is tender when pierced with a fork. Serve hot with the rice and garnish with parsley sprigs.

Cook's know-how

Do not let the sauce boil once you have added the mustard or it may taste bitter. Coarse-grain mustard gives an interesting texture to this dish, but if you prefer a smooth sauce, use Dijon mustard.

CORONATION CHICKEN

SERVES 6

1 tbsp sunflower oil
125g (4oz) spring onions, chopped
4 tsp mild curry paste
150ml (¼ pint) red wine
pared zest and juice of 1 lemon
1 tbsp tomato purée
2 tbsp apricot jam
300ml (½ pint) mayonnaise
150g (5oz) plain yogurt
salt and pepper
500g (1lb) cooked chicken,
   cut into bite-sized pieces
watercress sprigs to garnish
rice to serve

1 Heat the oil in a small saucepan, add the spring onions, and cook for about 2 minutes until beginning to soften but not colour. Stir in the curry paste, and cook, stirring, for 1 minute.

2 Add the red wine, lemon zest and juice, and tomato purée. Simmer, uncovered, stirring, for 5 minutes or until reduced to 4 tbsp. Strain into a bowl, cover, and leave to cool.

3 Work the apricot jam through the sieve, then stir it into the curry paste and wine mixture. Add the mayonnaise and yogurt, season with salt and pepper, then stir well to blend evenly. The mixture should have a coating consistency.

4 Add the chicken pieces to the mayonnaise mixture, and stir to coat evenly. Serve on a bed of rice and garnish with watercress sprigs before serving.

HERB-MARINATED CHICKEN BREASTS

SERVES 4

4 boneless chicken breasts,
  with the skin left on
30g (1oz) butter
2 tbsp sunflower oil
150ml (¼ pint) chicken stock
1 bunch of watercress, tough
  stalks removed, to serve
chopped parsley to garnish

MARINADE

2 tbsp olive oil
1 tbsp lemon juice
3 garlic cloves, crushed
3 tbsp chopped parsley
1 tbsp fresh herbs, chopped
salt and black pepper

1 Make the marinade: combine the oil, lemon juice, garlic, parsley, and fresh herbs, and season with salt and pepper. Turn the chicken in the marinade, cover, and leave to marinate in the refrigerator for at least 30 minutes.

2 Remove the chicken from the marinade, and dry on paper towels.

3 Melt the butter with the oil in a large frying pan. When the butter is foaming, add the chicken breasts, skin-side down, and cook for 10 minutes. Turn the chicken, and cook for a further 5 minutes or until golden and cooked through.

4 Using a slotted spoon, remove the chicken breasts, and keep hot.

5 Pour the chicken stock into the pan, and boil until reduced to about 8 tbsp.

6 Arrange the chicken breasts on beds of watercress, and strain over the hot sauce. Serve hot with mixed vegetables and garnished with chopped parsley.

> **Spicy chicken breasts**
>
> Substitute 1 tsp paprika and ¼ tsp crushed dried red chillies (chilli flakes) for the dried herbs in the marinade.

DUCK BREASTS WITH RASPBERRY SAUCE

SERVES 4

4 × 250–300g (8–10oz) duck breasts, with the skin left on
salt and black pepper
mixed vegetables to serve

RASPBERRY SAUCE

150ml (¼ pint) port
75ml (2½fl oz) water
45g (1½oz) caster sugar
250g (8oz) raspberries
1 tsp cornflour
juice of 2 oranges
salt and black pepper

1 Make the raspberry sauce: pour the port and measured water into a small saucepan. Add the sugar, and bring to a boil, stirring until the sugar has dissolved. Add the raspberries, bring back to a boil, then cover and simmer very gently for 5 minutes.

2 With a wooden spoon, push the raspberry mixture through a sieve to extract the seeds. Return the raspberry purée to the saucepan, and bring back to a boil.

3 Mix the cornflour with the orange juice. Add a little of the raspberry purée to the cornflour mixture, and blend together. Return to the saucepan, and bring back to a boil, stirring constantly until thickened. Season with salt and pepper, and set aside.

4 With a sharp knife, score the skin of each duck breast with criss-cross lines. Season both sides with salt and pepper.

5 Place the duck breasts under a hot grill, 10cm (4in) from the heat, and cook for 16 minutes, turning, or until the skin is crisp and the duck is tender but still slightly pink inside.

6 Slice the duck breasts, skin-side up, and arrange in a fan shape on warmed plates. Spoon raspberry sauce around each of the servings, and serve at once with vegetables of your choice.

CHEESE AND GARLIC STUFFED CHICKEN

SERVES 6

6 boneless chicken breasts,
  with the skin on
melted butter for brushing

STUFFING

30g (1oz) butter
1 onion, finely chopped
2 large garlic cloves, crushed
250g (8oz) full-fat soft cheese
1 tbsp chopped fresh tarragon
1 egg yolk
pinch of grated nutmeg
salt and black pepper

1 Make the stuffing: melt the butter in a small saucepan, add the onion and garlic, and cook gently, stirring occasionally, for a few minutes until soft but not coloured. Turn the onion mixture into a bowl, and leave to cool slightly.

2 Add the soft cheese to the onion mixture with the tarragon, egg yolk, and nutmeg. Season with salt and pepper and mix well.

3 Stuff the chicken breasts: lift up the skin along one side of each breast, spread the cheese mixture over the chicken and then gently press the skin back on top. Put the chicken breasts into an ovenproof dish and brush with the melted butter.

4 Roast the chicken in a preheated oven at 190°C (375°F, Gas 5) for 25–30 minutes until the chicken is cooked through. Cut each breast into diagonal slices, and serve hot with buttered carrot and courgette slices, cut with a potato peeler, and new potatoes.

Cook's know-how

Full-fat soft cheese is used here because it holds its shape well during cooking. Do not substitute a low-fat cheese because this will melt too quickly and make the chicken watery and soggy.

CHICKEN THIGHS NORMANDE

SERVES 4

3 leeks, trimmed and thinly sliced
4 lean back bacon rashers,
    rinds removed, diced
2 garlic cloves, crushed
350 ml (12 fl oz) strong dry cider
8 chicken thighs, with the bone
    in and skin left on
$1/2$ tsp chopped fresh thyme
salt and black pepper
125 ml (4 fl oz) crème fraîche
puréed butternut squash and
    mashed potato to serve

1 Put the leeks, bacon, and garlic into a roasting tin. Pour in the cider, and put the chicken on top. Sprinkle with the thyme, and season.

2 Roast in a preheated oven at 190°C (375°F, Gas 5) for 20–25 minutes until the chicken is tender and cooked through. Remove the chicken thighs, bacon, and vegetables, and keep warm.

3 Spoon off any excess fat from the roasting tin. Put the tin on the hob, and boil the cooking juices until reduced by half. Stir in the crème fraîche, and heat gently. Pour the sauce on to serving plates, arrange the bacon, vegetables, and chicken on top, and serve hot with puréed butternut squash and mashed potato.

ORIENTAL DUCK WITH GINGER

SERVES 4

4 × 250–300g (8–10oz) skinless
  duck breasts
1 tbsp sunflower oil
8 baby sweetcorn
bean sprouts and 1 tbsp toasted
  sesame seeds to garnish

MARINADE

200ml (7fl oz) orange juice
3 tbsp dark soy sauce
1 tbsp sesame oil
1 tbsp Chinese rice
  wine or dry sherry
1 tbsp clear honey
5cm (2in) piece of fresh root
  ginger, peeled nd grated
1 garlic clove, crushed
salt and black pepper

1 Make the marinade: in a large bowl, combine the orange juice, soy sauce, sesame oil, rice wine, honey, fresh root ginger, and garlic, then season with salt and pepper.

2 With a sharp knife, make several diagonal slashes in each duck breast. Pour the marinade over the duck breasts, turn them over, then cover and leave to marinate in the refrigerator for about 30 minutes.

3 Lift the duck breasts out of the marinade, reserving the marinade. Heat the oil in a large frying pan, add the duck breasts, and cook over a high heat, turning frequently, for 10–12 minutes until tender. Add the marinade and simmer for 2–3 minutes until slightly reduced.

4 Meanwhile, blanch the baby sweetcorn in boiling salted water for 1 minute. Drain, then make lengthways cuts in each one, leaving them attached at the stem.

5 To serve, slice each duck breast, and arrange on 4 individual plates. Spoon the hot sauce over the duck, add the sweetcorn, then garnish with bean sprouts and the toasted sesame seeds. Serve hot.

LEMON POUSSINS WITH ARTICHOKE HEARTS

SERVES 4

4 × 375g (12oz) poussins
salt and black pepper
4 garlic cloves
1 lemon, cut into quarters lengthways
4 rosemary sprigs
60g (2oz) butter, softened
1 × 300g (10oz) jar artichoke
  hearts in oil
175ml (6fl oz) dry white wine
fresh rosemary and lemon
  wedges to garnish

1 Season the poussins inside and out, and put a garlic clove, lemon quarter, and rosemary sprig into each one. Tie the legs together with string, then rub the birds with the softened butter.

2 Put the poussins upside down on a rack in a roasting tin. Roast in a preheated oven at 190°C (375°F, Gas 5) for 40–45 minutes, turning them the right way up halfway through.

3 While the poussins are roasting, drain the artichoke hearts, reserving 2–3 tbsp of the oil, and cut each artichoke heart in half.

4 Check the poussins are done by pricking with a fork – the juices should run clear, not pink or red. Remove them from the tin, and keep warm. Spoon off all but 1 tbsp fat from the tin, leaving behind the cooking juices.

5 Add the wine to the tin, mix with the juices, then boil on the hob until reduced to about 90ml (3fl oz).

6 Stir in the artichokes and the reserved oil, and heat through gently. Serve the poussins with the artichokes, sauce, and mashed potato, garnished with rosemary sprigs and lemon wedges.

TRADITIONAL ROAST PHEASANT

SERVES 4

2 pheasants, any giblets reserved
90g (3oz) butter, softened
salt and black pepper
4 streaky bacon rashers
1 tsp plain flour
300ml (½ pint) pheasant giblet
  (page 121) or chicken stock
1 tsp redcurrant jelly
watercress sprigs to garnish
game chips to serve (see below)

1 Spread the pheasants with the butter, and season. Lay two bacon rashers crossways over each breast.

2 Put the pheasants into a roasting tin, and cook in a preheated oven at 200°C (400°F, Gas 6), basting once, for 50 minutes to 1 hour or until tender.

3 Test the pheasants by inserting a fine skewer in the thickest part of a thigh: the juices should run clear when they are cooked.

4 Lift the pheasants on to a warmed serving platter, cover with foil, and keep warm. Pour off all but 1 tbsp of the fat from the roasting tin, reserving any juices. Put the tin on the hob, add the flour, and cook, stirring, for 1 minute.

5 Add the stock and redcurrant jelly, and bring to a boil, stirring until lightly thickened. Simmer for 2–3 minutes, then taste for seasoning. Strain into a warmed gravy boat.

6 To serve, garnish the pheasants with the watercress sprigs, and serve with fried breadcrumbs, game chips, bread sauce, and the gravy.

GAME CHIPS

Using a mandolin or the finest blade on a food processor, slice 500g (1lb) old potatoes finely, then dry them. Heat some sunflower oil in a deep-fat fryer, add the potato slices, and deep-fry for 3 minutes or until crisp and golden. Drain, then sprinkle with salt.

MUSHROOM-STUFFED QUAIL

SERVES 6

12 quail, boned
30g (1oz) butter, plus extra for greasing
1 tbsp lime marmalade

MUSHROOM STUFFING

60g (2oz) butter
3 shallots, finely chopped
375g (12oz) button mushrooms,
   coarsely chopped
60g (2oz) fresh white breadcrumbs
salt and black pepper
1 egg, beaten

LIME SAUCE

150ml (¼ pint) chicken stock
juice of 1 lime
200ml (7fl oz) full fat crème fraîche
4 tbsp chopped parsley

1 Make the mushroom stuffing: melt the butter in a saucepan, add the shallots, and cook gently, stirring occasionally, for 3–5 minutes until soft but not coloured.

2 Add the mushrooms and cook for 2 minutes, then remove from the heat. Stir in the breadcrumbs, season with salt and pepper, then stir in the egg and leave to cool. Spoon some of the stuffing into the cavity of each quail; secure the skin with a wooden cocktail stick.

3 Put the quail into a buttered roasting tin. Melt the butter gently in a saucepan, add the lime marmalade, and heat gently, stirring, until combined. Brush over the quail, and cook in a preheated oven at 200°C (400°F, Gas 6) for 15–20 minutes until golden brown and tender. Remove from the tin and keep warm.

4 Make the lime sauce: put the roasting tin on the hob. Add the stock, and bring to a boil, then stir for 5 minutes or until reduced a little.

5 Stir in the lime juice and crème fraîche, and heat gently, stirring constantly, until the sauce has a smooth, creamy consistency.

6 Add half of the parsley and season with salt and pepper. Serve the quail with the lime sauce, vegetables, and garnish with the remaining parsley.

PHEASANT STEW

SERVES 6–8

2 tbsp sunflower oil
2 pheasants, cut into serving pieces
375g (12oz) shallots, chopped
125g (4oz) piece of smoked
   streaky bacon, cut into strips
3 garlic cloves, crushed
1 tbsp plain flour
600ml (1 pint) pheasant giblet stock
   (see below), or use game
   stock or chicken stock
300ml (½ pint) red wine
1 head of celery, separated
   into stalks, sliced
250g (8oz) button mushrooms
1 tbsp tomato purée
salt and black pepper
red cabbage to serve

1 Heat the oil in a large flameproof casserole dish. Add the pheasant pieces and cook over a high heat until browned. Lift out and drain.

2 Add the shallots and bacon and cook for 5 minutes. Add the garlic and flour and cook, stirring, for 1 minute. Add the stock and wine and bring to a boil. Add the celery, mushrooms, tomato purée, and season. Simmer for 5 minutes.

3 Add the pheasant, bring back to a boil, cover, and cook in a preheated oven at 160°C (325°F, Gas 3) for about 2 hours. Serve with red cabbage.

PHEASANT GIBLET STOCK

Put the giblets (the neck, heart, and gizzard but not the liver) in a stockpot or large saucepan and cook until lightly browned. Stir in 1 litre (1¾ pints) water (or previously made stock). Bring to a boil, skimming off any scum that forms on the surface. Add 1–2 quartered, unpeeled onions, 1 chopped celery stalk, 1 chopped carrot, 1 bouquet garni, and a few black peppercorns. Simmer for about 1 hour. Strain, then cool, cover, and keep in the refrigerator for upto 3 days, or freeze for 3 months.

MARINATED CHICKEN WITH PEPPERS

SERVES 6

1.7kg (3½lb) chicken
2 tbsp olive oil
1 large red pepper, halved, seeded, and cut into thin strips
1 large yellow pepper, halved, seeded, and cut into thin strips
125g (4oz) pitted black olives

MARINADE

4 tbsp olive oil
2 tbsp clear honey
juice of ½ lemon
1 tbsp chopped mixed fresh herbs, such as parsley, thyme, and basil
salt and black pepper

1 Put the chicken into a roasting tin, rub the breast with oil, and roast in a preheated oven at 190°C (375°F, Gas 5) for 20 minutes per 500g (1lb). Twenty minutes before the end of the roasting time, remove from the oven, and spoon off the fat. Add the peppers and return to the oven for 20 minutes.

2 Remove the chicken and peppers from the tin, and leave to stand until cool.

3 Meanwhile, make the marinade: in a large bowl, combine the olive oil, honey, lemon juice, and herbs, and season with salt and pepper.

4 Strip the chicken flesh from the carcass, and cut it into small bite-sized strips. Toss the strips in the marinade, cover, and leave to cool completely.

5 Spoon the chicken on to a platter, arrange the peppers and olives around the edge, and serve at room temperature on a bed of lettuce leaves.

Cook's know-how

If time is short, use a ready-cooked chicken and toss with roasted peppers from a jar. If the peppers are packed in oil they will be very moist, so you will only need half the amount of marinade.

Meat

GRILLED PORK CHOPS WITH MANGO SAUCE

SERVES 4

4 pork loin chops, on the bone
sunflower oil for brushing
salt and black pepper
1 ripe mango
flat-leaf parsley to garnish

MANGO SAUCE

1 ripe mango
150ml (¼ pint) chicken stock
1 tbsp mango chutney

1 Cut through the fat at regular intervals on the edge of each pork chop (this will help prevent the chops from curling up during cooking).

2 Brush the chops on each side with oil and sprinkle with black pepper. Put under a hot grill, 10cm (4in) from the heat, and grill for 6 minutes on each side or until cooked through (timing depends on size of chops).

3 Meanwhile, make the mango sauce: peel, stone, and cube the mango, then purée in a food processor until smooth.

4 Put into a small saucepan with the stock, mango chutney, and salt and pepper. Bring to a boil and simmer for about 3 minutes until heated through. Taste for seasoning.

5 Peel the remaining mango and cut it into 2 pieces lengthwise, slightly off-centre to miss the stone. Cut the flesh from around the stone. Slice the flesh into thin strips.

6 Arrange the mango strips on the chops, garnish with flat-leaf parsley, and serve with the mango sauce, green beans, and wild rice.

CHÂTEAUBRIAND WITH BÉARNAISE SAUCE

SERVES 2

400g (13oz) Châteaubriand steak
(a thick piece of fillet from the
middle of the tenderloin)
30g (1oz) butter, melted
black pepper
béarnaise sauce (see below)

1 Cut the steak crossways in half. Brush one side of each half with melted butter and season with pepper.

2 Put the steaks, buttered-side up, under a hot grill, 7cm (3in) from the heat, and cook for 2 minutes or until browned. Turn the steaks over, brush with melted butter, and season with pepper. Grill for about 2 minutes until browned.

3 Lower the heat and cook, turning once and brushing with the butter, for 4–5 minutes. Cover and leave to stand for 5 minutes. Slice the steaks, and serve with the béarnaise sauce, green salad, and sautéed potato wedges.

BÉARNAISE SAUCE

Put 4 tbsp tarragon vinegar, 1 finely chopped shallot, and 1 tbsp chopped tarragon into a pan and boil for a few minutes until reduced by one-third. Leave to cool. Pour 2 egg yolks into a bowl over a saucepan of simmering water, add the vinegar mixture, and whisk over a gentle heat until thick and fluffy. Melt 90g (3oz) butter and gradually add to the sauce, whisking constantly until thick. Season with salt and white pepper.

TERIYAKI BEEF

SERVES 4

500g (1lb) rump steak, trimmed
  and cut into thin strips
2 tbsp sunflower oil
1 large onion, thinly sliced
1 red pepper, halved, seeded,
  and cut into strips
2 spring onions, sliced,
  to garnish

MARINADE

125ml (4fl oz) dark soy sauce
90ml (3fl oz) Japanese rice
  wine or dry sherry
2 tbsp caster sugar

1 Make the marinade: in a bowl, combine the soy sauce, rice wine, and sugar. Toss the steak strips in the marinade, cover, and leave to marinate in the refrigerator overnight.

2 Remove the steak strips from the marinade, reserving the marinade. Heat 1 tbsp of the oil in a wok, add the onion and red pepper, and stir-fry for about 2 minutes. Remove from the wok with a slotted spoon and set aside. Heat the remaining oil, and stir-fry the steak strips for 5 minutes or until just cooked through.

3 Return the onion and red pepper to the wok with the marinade and cook for 2 minutes or until heated through. Garnish with the spring onions before serving.

SERVES 6–8

2–2.5kg (4–5lb) leg of
  lamb, butterflied
roasted vegetables to serve

MARINADE

juice of 3 lemons
4 tbsp clear honey
3 large garlic cloves, quartered
2 tbsp coarse-grain mustard

LEMON-GRILLED LAMB

1 Make the marinade: in a non-metallic dish, mix together the lemon juice, honey, garlic, and mustard. Turn the lamb in the marinade, cover, and leave to marinate in the refrigerator, turning the lamb occasionally, for 1–2 days.

2 Remove the lamb from the marinade. Strain and reserve the marinade. Cook the lamb under a hot grill, about 15cm (6in) from the heat, basting from time to time with the marinade, for 20–25 minutes on each side.

3 Test the lamb: insert a skewer into the thickest part – the juices will run clear when it is cooked.

4 Leave the lamb to stand, covered with foil, in a warm place for 5–10 minutes. Spoon the fat from the grill pan, strain the juices into a gravy boat, and serve with the lamb and roasted vegetables.

Cook's know-how

Butterflied leg of lamb is a good cut for cooking on the barbecue as well as under the grill because the meat is thin enough to cook quickly without becoming too charred on the outside. The marinade in this recipe works equally well for lamb chops and cutlets, which can also be grilled or barbecued.

PORK WITH CHILLI AND COCONUT

SERVES 6

750g (1½lb) pork fillet (tenderloin), trimmed and cut into 5mm (¼in) strips
2 tbsp sunflower oil
8 spring onions, cut into 2.5cm (1in) pieces
1 large red pepper, halved, seeded, and cut into thin strips
1 × 400g (13oz) can chopped tomatoes
60g (2oz) creamed coconut, coarsely chopped
4 tbsp water
2 tbsp chopped fresh coriander
1 tbsp lemon juice
salt and black pepper
coriander sprigs to garnish
chinese noodles to serve

SPICE MIX

2.5cm (1in) piece of fresh root ginger, peeled and grated
2 fresh red chillies, halved, seeded, and finely chopped
1 garlic clove, crushed
1 tbsp mild curry powder

1 Make the spice mix: in a bowl, combine the ginger, chillies, garlic, and curry powder, and season with salt and pepper. Turn the pork in the mix, cover, and leave to marinate in the refrigerator for 2 hours.

2 Heat a wok or large frying pan, add the oil, and heat until hot. Add the strips of pork in batches, and stir-fry over a high heat for 5 minutes or until browned all over.

3 Add the spring onions and stir-fry for 1 minute. Add the red pepper and stir-fry for 1 minute, then add the tomatoes, coconut, and measured water. Bring to a boil, cover, and simmer very gently for 15 minutes or until the pork is tender.

4 Add the chopped coriander, lemon juice, and salt and pepper to taste. Garnish with coriander sprigs and serve on a bed of chinese noodles.

BOBOTIE

SERVES 6–8

1 slice of white bread, crusts removed
300ml (½ pint) milk
30g (1oz) butter
1 large onion, chopped
2 garlic cloves, crushed
1kg (2lb) raw minced beef
1 tbsp medium-hot curry powder
90g (3oz) ready-to-eat dried
  apricots, coarsely chopped
90g (3oz) blanched almonds,
  coarsely chopped
2 tbsp fruit chutney
1 tbsp lemon juice
salt and black pepper
2 eggs
30g (1oz) flaked almonds

1 Put the bread into a shallow dish. Sprinkle over 2 tbsp of the milk and leave to soak for 5 minutes.

2 Meanwhile, melt the butter in a large frying pan, add the onion and garlic, and cook gently, stirring occasionally, for a few minutes until soft.

3 Increase the heat, add the minced beef, and cook, stirring, for about 5 minutes or until browned. Spoon off any excess fat.

4 Add the curry powder and cook, stirring, for 2 minutes. Add the chopped apricots and almonds, the chutney, lemon juice, and salt and pepper to taste.

5 Mash the bread and milk in the dish, then stir into the minced beef. Turn into an ovenproof dish and bake in a preheated oven at 180°C (350°F, Gas 4) for 35 minutes.

6 Break the eggs into a bowl, and whisk in the remaining milk, and salt and pepper to taste. Pour over the minced beef mixture, sprinkle with the almonds, and bake for 25–30 minutes until the topping is set.

Healthy option

Almonds are the traditional topping for this South African recipe, but they can be omitted if you want to reduce the fat content of the dish.

SHOULDER OF LAMB WITH GARLIC AND HERBS

SERVES 6

2kg (4lb) shoulder of lamb,
 trimmed of excess fat
haricot beans to serve

HERB BUTTER

90g (3oz) butter, softened
2 garlic cloves, crushed
1 tbsp chopped fresh thyme
1 tbsp chopped fresh rosemary
1 tbsp chopped fresh mint
2 tbsp chopped parsley
salt and black pepper

GRAVY

1 tbsp plain flour
150ml (¼ pint) red wine
150ml (¼ pint) lamb or
 chicken stock

1 Make the herb butter: mix the butter, garlic, thyme, rosemary, mint, and parsley, and season with salt and pepper.

2 Slash the lamb at regular intervals with a sharp knife, then push the herb butter into the cuts. Rub any remaining butter over the lamb. Weigh the lamb.

3 Put the lamb on a rack in a roasting tin and insert a meat thermometer, if using, into the middle of the meat. Cook in a preheated oven at 200°C (400°F, Gas 6) for 30 minutes.

4 Lower the temperature to 180°C (350°F, Gas 4) and cook for 20 minutes per 500g (1lb). The thermometer should register 75–80°C (170–175°F).

5 Remove the lamb. Cover loosely with foil and leave to stand in a warm place for about 10 minutes.

6 Make the gravy: drain all but 1 tbsp of the fat from the tin. Set the tin on the hob, add the flour, and cook, stirring, for 1 minute. Pour in the wine and stock, bring to a boil, and simmer for 2–3 minutes. Taste for seasoning, and strain into a warmed gravy boat. Serve with the lamb and creamed haricot beans.

SERVES 6–8

1 × 750g (1½lb) bacon joint
a few parsley stalks
6 black peppercorns
1 bay leaf
4 potatoes, cut into large chunks
4 carrots, thickly sliced
4 celery stalks, thickly sliced
chopped parsley to garnish

CHEESE SAUCE

45g (1½oz) butter
45g (1½oz) plain flour
200ml (7fl oz) milk
90g (3oz) mature Cheddar cheese,
  grated salt and black pepper

FARMER'S BACON BAKE

1 Put the bacon joint into a large pan, cover with cold water, and bring to a boil. Drain, rinse, and cover with fresh cold water. Add the parsley stalks, peppercorns, and bay leaf, and bring to a boil. Cover and simmer very gently for 45 minutes.

2 Add the potatoes, carrots, and celery and bring back to a boil. Cover and simmer very gently for 20 minutes or until the meat and vegetables are tender. Drain, reserving the cooking liquid, and allow the bacon to cool slightly.

3 Remove the rind and fat from the bacon, cut the meat into bite-sized pieces, and place in a shallow baking dish with the vegetables. Keep hot.

4 Make the cheese sauce: melt the butter in a saucepan, sprinkle in the flour, and cook, stirring, for 1 minute. Remove from the heat and gradually blend in the milk and 250ml (8fl oz) of the reserved cooking liquid. Bring to a boil, stirring constantly until the mixture thickens. Simmer for 2–3 minutes. Add three-quarters of the cheese, and season.

5 Pour the sauce over the meat and vegetables and sprinkle with the remaining cheese. Bake in a preheated oven at 180°C (350°F, Gas 4) for 30 minutes or until the cheese topping is bubbling. Garnish with chopped parsley before serving.

THAI RED BEEF CURRY

SERVES 6

3 tbsp sunflower oil

8 cardamom pods, split

2.5cm (1in) piece of cinnamon stick

6 cloves

8 black peppercorns

1kg (2lb) braising steak, trimmed
  and cut into 2.5cm (1in) cubes

1 large onion, chopped

5cm (2in) piece of fresh root
  ginger, peeled and grated

4 garlic cloves, crushed

4 tsp paprika

2 tsp ground cumin

1 tsp ground coriander

1 tsp salt

$\frac{1}{4}$ tsp cayenne pepper
  or $\frac{1}{2}$ tsp chilli powder

600ml (1 pint) water

90g (3oz) full-fat plain yogurt

1 × 400g (13oz) can chopped tomatoes

1 large red pepper, halved, seeded,
  and cut into chunks

rice to serve

1 Heat the oil in a large flameproof casserole, add the cardamom pods, cinnamon stick, cloves, and peppercorns, and cook over a moderate heat, stirring, for 1 minute. Lift out with a slotted spoon and set aside on a plate.

2 Add the beef in batches, and cook over a high heat until browned all over. Lift out the beef with a slotted spoon and drain on paper towels.

3 Add the onion to the pan and cook over a high heat, stirring, for about 3 minutes until beginning to brown. Add the ginger, garlic, paprika, cumin, coriander, salt, cayenne or chilli, and 4 tbsp of the measured water. Cook, stirring, for about 1 minute.

4 Return the beef and spices to the casserole, then gradually add the yogurt, stirring. Stir in the remaining water. Add the tomatoes and red pepper, and bring to a boil. Cover and cook in a preheated oven at 160°C (325°F, Gas 3) for 2 hours or until the beef is tender. Taste for seasoning before serving with boiled rice.

Cook's know-how

If you are short of time, use 3–4 tbsp ready made Thai red curry paste instead of the whole and ground spices in this recipe. If you prefer, you can use coconut milk instead of the yogurt.

BOSTON BAKED BEANS

SERVES 6–8

375g (12oz) dried haricot beans
60g (2oz) dark muscovado sugar
2 tbsp tomato purée
2 tsp black treacle
2 tsp golden syrup
2 tsp mustard powder
2 tsp salt
black pepper
250g (8oz) piece of streaky bacon, cut into 2.5cm (1in) cubes
3 onions, quartered
600ml (1 pint) water

1 Put the haricot beans into a large bowl, cover with plenty of cold water, and leave to soak overnight.

2 Drain the beans, and rinse under cold running water. Put the beans into a saucepan, cover with cold water, and bring to a boil. Boil rapidly for 10 minutes, then partially cover the pan and simmer for 30 minutes. Drain and set aside.

3 Put the sugar, tomato purée, black treacle, golden syrup, and mustard powder into a large flameproof casserole. Season with salt and pepper and heat gently, stirring constantly.

4 Add the bacon and onions to the casserole with the drained beans and measured water. Bring to a boil, cover tightly, and cook in a preheated oven at 140°C (275°F, Gas 1), stirring occasionally, for 4½-5 hours. Taste for seasoning before serving.

Healthy option

Boston baked beans traditionally contain belly pork or bacon, which makes the dish quite high in fat. Without the pork or bacon, the beans make a tasty vegetarian main course that is much lower in fat, and if you serve it with crusty bread and a leafy green salad it makes a well-balanced, nutritious meal.

SERVES 8

1.5kg (3lb) boned and rolled veal
   roasting joint, such as loin
2 large rosemary sprigs
2 garlic cloves, cut into slivers
salt and black pepper
250ml (8fl oz) dry white wine

TUNA MAYONNAISE

1 × 200g (7oz) can tuna in oil, drained
2 tbsp lemon juice
1 garlic clove, crushed
2 tbsp capers
1 tsp chopped fresh thyme
dash of Tabasco sauce
125ml (4fl oz) olive oil
250ml (8fl oz) mayonnaise

TO GARNISH

black olives
1 red pepper, halved, seeded,
   and cut into strips
fresh basil

VEAL WITH TUNA MAYONNAISE

1 Make incisions in the veal and push 1 or 2 rosemary leaves and a sliver of garlic into each incision. Season, and rub with any remaining rosemary and garlic.

2 Place the veal in a large roasting tin and pour the wine around it. Cover with foil and roast in a preheated oven at 160°C (325°F, Gas 3) for 2–2½ hours or until tender.

3 Remove the veal from the oven, and leave to cool completely in the cooking liquid. Remove any fat that solidifies on the surface. Slice the veal thinly and arrange the slices on a serving platter.

4 Make the tuna mayonnaise: purée the tuna, reserving a little for the garnish, with the lemon juice, garlic, capers, thyme, and Tabasco sauce in a food processor until smooth. Gradually blend in the oil, then add the mayonnaise, and season with salt and pepper. Pour over the veal. At this stage you can garnish and serve, or cover and refrigerate overnight to serve the next day.

5 To serve, garnish with the reserved tuna, the black olives, red pepper, and basil. Serve at room temperature (if refrigerated overnight, take it out for about 1 hour before serving).

MUSTARD-GLAZED HAM

SERVES 16–20

4–5kg (8–10lb) smoked gammon
400ml (14fl oz) cider or apple juice
3 tbsp English mustard
90g (3oz) demerara sugar

LEMON MUSTARD SAUCE

4 tbsp olive oil
juice of 1 lemon
1 tbsp caster sugar
2 tsp coarse-grain mustard
salt and black pepper
150ml (¼ pint) crème fraîche

GLAZING HAM

Cut away the skin with a sharp knife, leaving behind a thin layer of fat. Discard the skin. Score the fat all over in a diamond pattern, so that the glaze penetrates the fat. Spread a generous layer of mustard over the fat, using a palette knife or your hands. Press the demerara sugar on to the layer of mustard, making sure it is evenly coated all over.

1 Put the gammon into a large container, cover with cold water, and leave for 12 hours. Drain and rinse. Arrange 2 pieces of foil, long enough to cover the gammon, across a large roasting tin. Pour the cider into the foil, stand a wire rack on top, and stand the gammon on the rack. Insert a meat thermometer, if using, into the thickest part of the meat.

2 Wrap the foil loosely over the gammon, leaving plenty of space for air to circulate. Place the gammon just below the middle of a preheated oven and cook at 160°C (325°F, Gas 3) for 20 minutes per 500g (1lb). The meat thermometer should register 75°C (170°F). Remove the ham from the oven and leave to cool for a few minutes. Increase the oven temperature to 230°C (450°F, Gas 8). Transfer the ham to a board, drain the cooking juices from the foil, and discard. Glaze the gammon with the mustard and sugar (see left).

3 Return the ham to the rack in the roasting tin. Cover any lean parts with foil, return to the oven, and cook, turning the roasting tin if necessary, for 15–20 minutes until the glaze is golden brown all over.

4 Meanwhile, make the lemon mustard sauce: put the oil, lemon juice, sugar, and mustard into a screw-top jar, season, and shake vigorously. Put the crème fraîche into a bowl and stir in the mustard mixture. Taste for seasoning and chill until needed. Carve the ham into slices and serve either warm or cold, with the lemon mustard sauce.

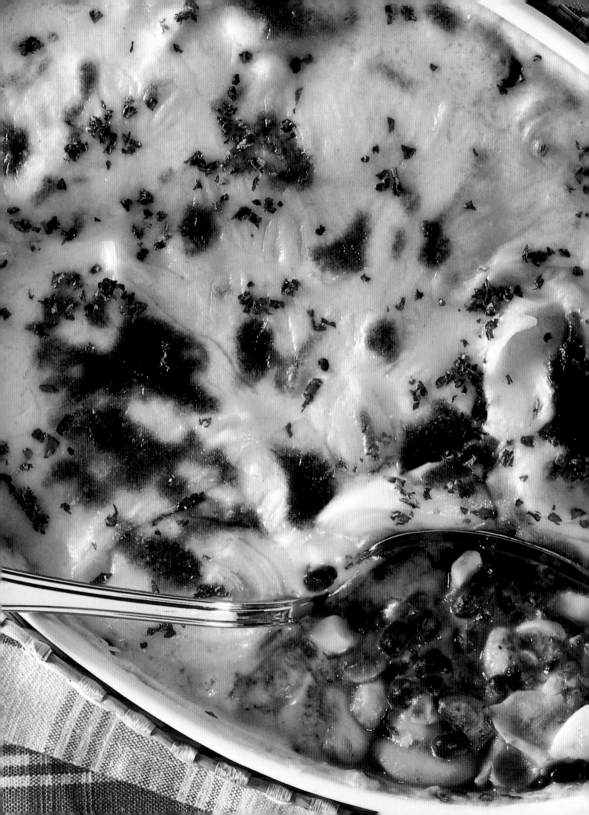

Vegetarian Mains

SERVES 4–6

23CM (9IN) FLAN DISH OR TIN
BAKING BEANS

30g (1oz) butter
175g (6oz) leeks, trimmed
  and finely sliced
250g (8oz) young spinach
  leaves, coarsely chopped
2 eggs, beaten
150ml (¼ pint) each double cream
  and milk, or 300ml (½ pint) full
  cream milk
90g (3oz) Gruyère cheese, grated
salt and black pepper

SHORTCRUST PASTRY

175g (6oz) plain flour
90g (3oz) butter
about 2 tbsp cold water

SPINACH, LEEK, AND GRUYÈRE TART

1 Make the pastry: tip the flour into a bowl and rub in the butter with your fingertips. Add enough water to bind to a soft dough.

2 Roll out the pastry on a lightly floured work surface, and use to line the flan dish or tin. Prick the bottom of the pastry case with a fork. Chill in the refrigerator for 30 minutes.

3 Line the pastry case with foil or greaseproof paper, and fill with baking beans (or rice or pasta if you have no beans). Put the dish or tin on a heated baking tray, and bake in a preheated oven at 220°C (425°F, Gas 7) for 15–20 minutes, removing the foil and beans for the final 10 minutes.

4 Make the filling: melt the butter in a frying pan, add the leeks, and cook over a high heat for 5 minutes or until just beginning to turn golden brown. Add the spinach and cook for about 2 minutes until it just begins to wilt. Spoon the filling into the pastry case.

5 Mix together the eggs, milk, cream, and Gruyère cheese in a jug, season with salt and pepper, and pour into the pastry case.

6 Reduce the oven temperature to 180°C (350°F, Gas 4), and bake for 25 minutes or until the filling is golden and set. Serve warm or cold.

EGGS FLORENTINE

SERVES 4

4 FLAMEPROOF DISHES

250g (8oz) spinach leaves
3 spring onions, thinly sliced
2 tbsp double cream
4 eggs
3 tbsp grated Parmesan cheese

CHEESE SAUCE

30g (1oz) butter
30g (1oz) plain flour
250ml (8fl oz) milk
175g (6oz) mature Cheddar
  cheese, grated
pinch each of cayenne pepper
  and grated nutmeg
salt and black pepper

1 Rinse the spinach, and put into a saucepan with only the water that clings to the leaves. Cook for about 2 minutes until tender. Drain, and set aside.

2 Make the cheese sauce: melt the butter in a saucepan, add the flour, and cook, stirring, for 1 minute. Remove from the heat and gradually blend in the milk. Bring to a boil, stirring constantly until the mixture thickens. Simmer for 2–3 minutes. Stir in the Cheddar cheese, add the cayenne pepper and nutmeg, and season. Keep warm.

3 Combine the spinach in a bowl with the spring onions and cream, and season. Set aside.

4 Poach the eggs: bring a large pan of water to a boil. Lower the heat so that the water is simmering, and slide in the eggs, one at a time. Swirl the water round the eggs to make neat shapes. Lift out with a slotted spoon.

5 Divide the spinach and spring onion mixture among 4 warmed flameproof dishes. Arrange the poached eggs on the spinach, and spoon the cheese sauce over the eggs.

6 Sprinkle the grated Parmesan cheese over the sauce, then place the dishes under a hot grill, 7cm (3in) from the heat, until the cheese has melted and is lightly browned, and the whole dish is heated through. Serve hot.

COUSCOUS WITH ROASTED PEPPERS

SERVES 4–6

1 large red pepper
1 large yellow pepper
175g (6oz) couscous
600ml (1 pint) hot vegetable stock
2 tbsp olive oil
60g (2oz) blanched almonds
2 courgettes, sliced
1 large red onion, chopped
1 large carrot, thinly sliced
1–2 garlic cloves, crushed
1 × 400g (13oz) can chick peas,
  drained and rinsed
1 tsp ground cumin
½ tsp curry powder
¼-½ tsp crushed dried red chillies
salt and black pepper
chopped coriander to garnish

1 Cook the peppers under a hot grill, 10cm (4in) from the heat, for 10 minutes or until charred. Seal in a plastic bag and leave to cool.

2 Put the couscous into a bowl and stir in the hot stock. Cover and leave to stand for 10 minutes.

3 Meanwhile, heat the oil in a large frying pan, add the almonds, and cook gently, stirring, for 3 minutes or until lightly browned. Lift out with a slotted spoon and drain on paper towels.

4 Add the courgettes, onion, carrot, and garlic to the pan, and cook, stirring, for about 5 minutes.

5 Stir in the chick peas, cumin, curry powder, and crushed chillies, and cook, stirring occasionally, for a further 5 minutes. Stir in the couscous, and cook for 3–4 minutes until heated through. Season to taste.

6 Remove the skins, cores, and seeds from the grilled peppers, and cut the flesh into thin strips.

7 Divide the couscous among warmed serving plates and arrange the pepper strips on top. Serve at once, sprinkled with the almonds and chopped coriander.

MEXICAN CHILLI WITH TOFU

SERVES 6

3 onions, chopped
3 garlic cloves, roughly chopped
1 fresh green chilli, halved, seeded,
   and roughly chopped
2 tsp paprika
1 tbsp mild chilli powder
4 tbsp sunflower oil
1 × 400g (13oz) can chopped tomatoes,
   drained and juice reserved
500ml (16fl oz) hot vegetable stock
625g (1¼lb) firm tofu, cut into
   bite-sized pieces
1 × 400g (13oz) can red kidney
   beans, drained
salt and black pepper
chopped fresh coriander to garnish
rice and nachos to serve

1 Put the onions, garlic, green chilli, and spices into a food processor and process until fairly chunky.

2 Heat the oil in a large frying pan. Add the onion mixture and cook for a few minutes, stirring occasionally, until softened and fragrant.

3 Add the tomatoes to the pan and cook, stirring occasionally, until reduced and thickened. Pour in the stock and cook for 5–10 minutes more until thickened again.

4 Add the tofu, kidney beans, and the reserved tomato juice, and cook, spooning the sauce over the tofu pieces, for 5–8 minutes until heated through. Do not stir the tofu as it may break up. Season with salt and pepper, and serve hot, with the rice and nachos, sprinkled with coriander.

Cook's know-how

Reducing a sauce involves cooking it over a high heat to allow the moisture to evaporate and the flavours to become concentrated.

RED BEAN AND TOMATO CURRY

SERVES 4

2 tbsp sunflower oil
1 large onion, sliced
3 garlic cloves, crushed
1–2 fresh green chillies,
  halved, seeded, and sliced
2.5cm (1in) piece of fresh root
  ginger, peeled and grated
1 tbsp Madras or other hot curry powder
salt
1 × 400g (13oz) can chopped tomatoes
2 × 400g (13oz) cans red kidney
  beans, drained and rinsed
1 tbsp lemon juice
fresh coriander leaves to garnish
toasted naan bread to serve

1 Heat the oil in a large frying pan, add the onion, garlic, chillies, and ginger, and cook, stirring occasionally, for a few minutes until all the aromas are released, and the onion is soft but not coloured.

2 Add the curry powder and season with salt, then cook, stirring, for 2 minutes.

3 Add the tomatoes with most of their juice and cook for about 3 minutes. Add the beans and cook for a further 5 minutes or until the beans are warmed through and the sauce is thickened. Add the lemon juice and serve hot, garnished with coriander and serve with toasted naan bread.

SPINACH AND RICOTTA SAMOSAS

SERVES 4

4 sheets of filo pastry
60g (2oz) melted butter,
  plus extra for greasing

FILLING

30g (1oz) butter
1 small onion, finely chopped
300g (10oz) spinach, shredded
125g (4oz) ricotta cheese
pinch of grated nutmeg
salt and black pepper

TOMATO SAUCE

30g (1oz) butter
1 small onion, chopped
1 small carrot, chopped
30g (1oz) plain flour
1 × 400g (13oz) can chopped tomatoes
300ml (1/2 pint) vegetable stock
1 bay leaf
1 tsp caster sugar

1 Make the filling: melt the butter in a saucepan, add the onion, and cook gently over a medium heat for 3–5 minutes until softened. Add the spinach to the onion and cook for 1–2 minutes. Leave to cool. Add the ricotta and nutmeg, season with salt and pepper, and mix well. Divide into 8 portions.

2 Lightly butter a baking tray. Cut each sheet of filo pastry lengthways into 2 long strips. Brush 1 strip with melted butter, covering the remaining strips with a damp tea towel.

3 Fill and fold the parcels: spoon 1 portion of filling on to a corner of the filo strip. Fold over opposite corners to form a triangle. Fold the filled triangle until you reach the end of the strip. Brush with melted butter and put on to the baking tray. Butter, fill, and fold the remaining filo strips.

4 Make the tomato sauce: melt the butter in a pan, add the onion and carrot, and cook for 10 minutes or until softened. Sprinkle in the flour and cook, stirring, for 1 minute. Add the tomatoes, stock, bay leaf, and sugar, season with salt and pepper, and bring to a boil. Cover and simmer for 30 minutes. Purée in a food processor until smooth. Keep hot.

5 Bake the parcels in a preheated 200°C (400°F, Gas 6) oven for 20 minutes. Serve with the tomato sauce.

MIXED BEAN BAKE

SERVES 6

2 tbsp olive oil
3 large leeks, trimmed and sliced
1 garlic clove, crushed
250g (8oz) mushrooms, sliced
1 × 400g (13oz) can aduki or red
  kidney beans, drained and rinsed
1 × 400g (13oz) can butter beans,
  drained and rinsed
1 × 400g (13oz) can chopped tomatoes
3 tbsp tomato purée
4 tbsp chopped parsley
salt and black pepper

CHEESE SAUCE

30g (1oz) butter
30g (1oz) plain flour
300ml (½ pint) milk
1 egg, beaten
125g (4oz) Cheddar cheese, grated

1 Heat the olive oil in a large saucepan. Add the leeks and cook gently, stirring, for a few minutes until softened but not coloured. Lift out with a slotted spoon and set aside.

2 Add the garlic and mushrooms and cook, stirring occasionally, for about 5 minutes. Add the canned beans, tomatoes, tomato purée, and 3 tbsp of the parsley. Season with salt and pepper. Bring to a boil, cover, and simmer very gently for about 20 minutes.

3 Meanwhile, make the cheese sauce: melt the butter in a small saucepan, add the flour, and cook, stirring, for 1 minute. Remove the pan from the heat and gradually blend in the milk. Bring to a boil, stirring constantly until the mixture thickens. Simmer for 2–3 minutes, then leave to cool slightly. Stir in the egg and cheese, and season.

4 Transfer the bean mixture to an ovenproof dish and arrange the leeks on top. Pour the cheese sauce over the leeks, and bake in a preheated oven at 190°C (375°F, Gas 5) for 30 minutes or until the top is golden. Serve hot, sprinkled with the remaining parsley.

POLENTA WITH GRILLED VEGETABLES

SERVES 6

175g (6oz) polenta
150ml (¼ pint) cold water
600ml (1 pint) boiling salted water
30g (1oz) butter
2 courgettes, halved and
   thickly sliced lengthways
2 tomatoes, cored and sliced
1 fennel bulb, trimmed and
   quartered lengthways
1 red onion, thickly sliced
melted butter for brushing

MARINADE

4 tbsp olive oil
2 tbsp red wine vinegar
3 garlic cloves, chopped
2–3 tbsp chopped parsley
salt and black pepper

1 Put the polenta into a saucepan, cover with the measured cold water, and leave to stand for 5 minutes.

2 Add the boiling salted water to the pan, return to a boil, and stir for 10–15 minutes, until smooth and thickened.

3 Sprinkle a baking tray with water. Stir the butter into the polenta, then spread the mixture over the tray in a 1cm (½in) layer. Leave to cool.

4 Combine the marinade ingredients in a bowl. Add the courgettes, tomatoes, fennel, and onion. Cover and marinate in the refrigerator for 30 minutes.

5 Lift the vegetables out of the marinade and cook over a hot barbecue for 2–3 minutes on each side. Cut the polenta into strips and cook over a hot barbecue, brushing with melted butter, for 1–2 minutes on each side until golden. Serve hot.

Cook's know-how

Instead of barbecuing the polenta and vegetables, you can cook them on a ridged cast-iron chargrill pan, or under a preheated grill, for the same length of time.

SERVES 6–8

1KG (2LB) LOAF TIN

75g (2½oz) brown rice
salt and black pepper
15g (½oz) dried ceps
30g (1oz) butter
2 carrots, grated
1 small onion, finely chopped
1 garlic clove, crushed
250g (8oz) button mushrooms, chopped
2 tbsp chopped parsley
1 tbsp chopped fresh rosemary
125g (4oz) walnuts, toasted
  and chopped
125g (4oz) Brazil nuts, toasted
  and chopped
60g (2oz) pine nuts, toasted
175g (6oz) Cheddar cheese, grated
1 egg, beaten
sunflower oil for greasing
rosemary sprigs to garnish
cranberry sauce (see below) to serve

NUT LOAF

1 Cook the rice in boiling salted water for 30–35 minutes until tender.

2 Meanwhile, soak the ceps in a bowl of warm water for about 20–30 minutes.

3 Drain the rice when it is ready. Drain the ceps, pat dry, and chop finely.

4 Melt the butter in a frying pan, add the carrots, onion, and garlic, and cook gently, stirring occasionally, for 5 minutes. Stir in the chopped mushrooms, rice, ceps, parsley, and rosemary, and cook until softened.

5 Purée the mixture in a food processor. Stir in the walnuts, Brazil nuts, pine nuts, cheese, and egg. Season with salt and pepper.

6 Lightly grease the loaf tin, spoon in the mixture, and level the top. Cover with foil and bake in a preheated oven at 190°C (375°F, Gas 5) for 1½ hours or until firm. Turn out, cut into slices, and garnish. Serve hot, with cranberry sauce.

CRANBERRY SAUCE

Put 500g (1lb) fresh cranberries into a saucepan with 125ml (4fl oz) water. Bring to a boil and simmer for about 5 minutes, until the cranberries have begun to break down. Stir in 125g (4oz) caster sugar and simmer until the sugar has dissolved. Stir in 2 tbsp port before serving. Serve hot or cold.

Pasta and Rice Mains

PASTA ALLA MARINARA

SERVES 6

500g (1lb) pasta bows
salt and black pepper
2 tbsp olive oil
1 large onion, finely chopped
1 large garlic clove, crushed
125ml (4fl oz) dry white wine
125g (4oz) squid, cut into strips or rings
60g (2oz) button mushrooms, sliced
125g (4oz) scallops, halved
125g (4oz) cooked peeled prawns
150ml (¼ pint) double cream
4 tbsp chopped parsley

1 Cook the pasta bows in a large saucepan of boiling salted water for 8–10 minutes until just tender.

2 Meanwhile, heat the oil in a large pan, add the onion and garlic, and cook gently, stirring occasionally, for 3–5 minutes until softened but not coloured.

3 Pour in the white wine and boil to reduce the liquid in the saucepan to about 2 tbsp, stirring constantly. Add the squid and cook for 1 minute, then add the mushrooms and scallops, and cook, stirring, for a further 2 minutes. Add the prawns, cream, and half of the parsley, and heat through.

4 Drain the pasta bows thoroughly, and add to the seafood mixture, stirring well to combine. Season with salt and black pepper, and serve at once, garnished with the remaining chopped parsley.

Healthy option

Seafood and cream are a classic combination for a pasta sauce, but you may prefer a slightly less rich alternative. In fact, you can omit the cream altogether and use a few tablespoons of the pasta cooking water instead. Italian cooks often use this technique.

SERVES 6

125g (4oz) goat's cheese,
   cut into small pieces
3 tbsp olive oil
3 garlic cloves, crushed
3 tbsp shredded fresh basil
500g (1lb) penne or spaghetti
salt and black pepper
500g (1lb) asparagus

PENNE WITH ASPARAGUS

1 In a small bowl, combine the goat's cheese, olive oil, garlic, and shredded fresh basil.

2 Cook the pasta in a large saucepan of boiling salted water for 8–10 minutes until just tender.

3 Meanwhile, trim any woody ends from the asparagus and peel the spears if they are not young. Cut the asparagus into bite-sized pieces and cook in boiling salted water for about 3 minutes until just tender.

4 Drain the pasta thoroughly, add the goat's cheese mixture, and toss together. Drain the asparagus and add to the pasta mixture. Toss lightly together, season with salt and black pepper, and serve at once.

TORTELLINI WITH PEAS AND BACON

SERVES 6

500g (1lb) tortellini
salt and black pepper
1 tbsp sunflower oil
250g (8oz) bacon or pancetta rashers, any rinds removed, diced
175g (6oz) frozen petits pois
300ml (½ pint) double cream
grated Parmesan cheese to serve

1 Cook the tortellini in boiling salted water for about 10–12 minutes, or according to packet instructions, until tender.

2 Meanwhile, heat the oil in a frying pan, add the bacon, and cook over a high heat, stirring, for 3 minutes or until crisp.

3 Cook the petits pois in boiling salted water for about 2 minutes until just tender. Drain.

4 Drain the tortellini thoroughly and return to the saucepan. Add the bacon, petits pois, cream, and nutmeg, and season with salt and pepper. Heat gently for 1–2 minutes to warm through. Serve at once, sprinkled with grated Parmesan cheese.

Healthy option

Use just 150ml (¼ pint) low-fat crème fraîche instead of the double cream. Then do what the Italians do – splash a few ladlefuls of the pasta water into the sauce and stir vigorously to make enough sauce to coat the pasta.

KEDGEREE

SERVES 4

175g (6oz) long grain rice
1 tsp turmeric
375g (12oz) smoked haddock fillet
2 hard-boiled eggs
60g (2oz) butter, plus extra for greasing
juice of ½ lemon
150ml (¼ pint) single cream
salt
cayenne pepper
2 tbsp finely chopped parsley

1 Simmer the rice and turmeric, covered, in boiling salted water for 12–15 minutes until tender. Rinse with boiling water, drain, and keep warm.

2 Meanwhile, put the haddock, skin-side down, in a frying pan, cover with cold water, and poach for 8–10 minutes.

3 Cut 1 egg lengthways into quarters and reserve for garnish. Coarsely chop the second egg.

4 Drain the haddock, remove the skin and bones, then flake the fish. Put the fish into a large bowl, add the rice, chopped egg, butter, lemon juice, and cream, and season with salt and cayenne pepper. Stir gently to mix.

5 Butter an ovenproof dish, add the kedgeree, and bake in a preheated oven at 180°C (350°F, Gas 4), stirring occasionally, for 10–15 minutes.

6 To serve, stir in the parsley and garnish with the reserved egg quarters.

Cook's know-how

Some smoked haddock is dyed bright yellow, so look out for smoked haddock that is pale in colour and labelled "undyed" if you want to avoid artificial colourings.

FETTUCCINE PRIMAVERA

SERVES 4

125g (4oz) asparagus, trimmed
and cut into bite-sized pieces
125g (4oz) broccoli florets
1 courgette, sliced
salt and black pepper
3 tbsp olive oil
½ red and ½ yellow pepper,
halved, seeded, and diced
3 garlic cloves, crushed
1 × 200g (7oz) can chopped tomatoes
90g (3oz) frozen petits pois
125ml (4fl oz) double cream
500g (1lb) fettuccine
4 tbsp shredded fresh basil
90g (3oz) Parmesan cheese,
grated, to serve

1 Cook the asparagus, broccoli, and courgette in boiling salted water for 3 minutes or until just tender. Drain, rinse under cold running water, and set aside.

2 Heat the oil in a large, deep frying pan, add the peppers and garlic, and cook, stirring, for 4 minutes or until the peppers are softened.

3 Add the tomatoes and the petits pois, and cook for 5 minutes or until the liquid in the pan is reduced by about a half.

4 Add the asparagus, broccoli, and courgette, stir in the cream, and boil for 1–2 minutes to reduce the liquid and concentrate the flavour. Add salt and pepper to taste, and remove from the heat.

5 Cook the fettuccine in a large saucepan of boiling salted water for 8–10 minutes until just tender.

6 Drain the fettuccine thoroughly, add to the sauce, and toss over a high heat. Stir in the shredded basil and serve at once, sprinkled with Parmesan cheese.

Healthy option

For a lighter, less creamy, version of this classic dish, use 1 × 400g (13oz) can chopped tomatoes and omit the cream. Instead of sprinkling with Parmesan to serve, sprinkle with more shredded fresh basil.

RISOTTO MILANESE

SERVES 6

90g (3oz) butter
1 onion, chopped
375g (12oz) risotto rice
1.25 litres (2 pints) hot vegetable
  or chicken stock
a few pinches of saffron strands
salt and black pepper
60g (2oz) Parmesan cheese, grated
Parmesan shavings to serve

1 Melt 30g (1oz) of the butter in a large saucepan, add the chopped onion, and cook gently over a medium heat, stirring occasionally, for 3–5 minutes until softened but not coloured.

2 Add the rice, stirring to coat the grains in the butter, and cook for 1 minute. Add a ladleful of hot stock to the pan, and cook gently, stirring constantly, until all the stock has been absorbed.

3 Sprinkle in the saffron strands and season with salt and pepper. Continue to add the stock, a ladleful at a time, stirring constantly, until the risotto is thick and creamy and the rice tender. This will take about 20–25 minutes.

4 Stir in the remaining butter and the Parmesan cheese, and season to taste with salt and pepper. Serve at once, topped with Parmesan shavings.

Cook's know-how

Risotto milanese is the traditional accompaniment to Osso buco, but you can serve it with any other dish of meat or poultry, or as a first course on its own. In the past, it was traditionally cooked with the marrow from the veal shanks used for the osso buco, but nowadays the finished risotto is sometimes topped with a few spoonfuls of the juices from a veal roast to give it a more traditional and authentic flavour. If you want to reduce the fat content in this recipe, omit the butter in step 4.

SERVES 6–8

375g (12oz) short-cut macaroni
salt and black pepper
45g (1½oz) butter, plus extra for greasing
45g (1½oz) plain flour
900ml (1½ pints) milk
2 tsp Dijon mustard
175g (6oz) smoked Cheddar
    cheese, grated
60g (2oz) light mozzarella cheese, grated
90g (3oz) mature Cheddar cheese, grated
60g (2oz) fresh white breadcrumbs
tomato and onion salad to serve

THREE-CHEESE MACARONI

1 Cook the macaroni in boiling salted water for 8–10 minutes until just tender. Drain and set aside.

2 Melt the butter in a large saucepan. Add the flour and cook, stirring, for 1 minute. Remove the pan from the heat and gradually blend in the milk. Bring to a boil, stirring constantly until the mixture thickens. Simmer for about 5 minutes, stirring.

3 Stir in the mustard, smoked Cheddar and mozzarella cheeses, 60g (2oz) of the mature Cheddar cheese, and the cooked macaroni. Season with salt and pepper.

4 Lightly butter a large shallow ovenproof dish and spoon in the macaroni mixture. Sprinkle with the breadcrumbs and the remaining Cheddar cheese and bake in a preheated oven at 200°C (400°F, Gas 6) for about 15–20 minutes until golden and bubbling. Serve with a tomato and onion salad.

Cheese and leek macaroni

Omit the mozzarella cheese. Melt 30g (1oz) butter in a saucepan, add 2–3 trimmed and finely sliced leeks, and cook gently for 3–5 minutes until softened. Add the leeks to the sauce with the two Cheddar cheeses and the cooked and drained macaroni.

TAGLIATELLE WITH VEGETABLE RIBBONS

SERVES 4

375g (12oz) courgettes
250g (8oz) carrots, peeled
salt
375g (12oz) fresh tagliatelle
scant 1 tbsp olive oil
1 garlic clove, crushed
200ml (7fl oz) half-fat crème fraîche
2 tbsp ready made pesto
60g (2oz) dolcelatte cheese
chopped parsley to garnish

1 Thinly slice the courgettes and carrots into wide, thin ribbons.

2 Bring a large pan of salted water to a boil, add the tagliatelle, courgettes, and carrots, and cook for 3 minutes. Drain and refresh under cold running water.

3 Heat the oil in a large frying pan, add the garlic, and stir-fry for about 1 minute.

4 Add the crème fraîche and pesto, then crumble in the cheese. Simmer and stir the sauce for 2–3 minutes, then add the tagliatelle and vegetables. Mix gently, turn into a warmed serving dish, and sprinkle with chopped parsley. Serve immediately.

Cook's know-how

Dolcelatte is a mild and creamy blue cheese from Italy. For a change you could use gorgonzola, another Italian blue cheese which has a stronger, saltier flavour. The French Roquefort could also be used.

SERVES 8

625g (1¼lb) haddock fillet
1 slice of onion
1 bay leaf
4 black peppercorns
300ml (½ pint) dry white wine
250g (8oz) cooked peeled prawns
30g (1oz) butter
500g (1lb) courgettes, thickly sliced
1 garlic clove, crushed
175g (6oz) pre-cooked lasagne sheets
60g (2oz) Cheddar cheese, grated
2 tbsp grated Parmesan cheese

SAUCE

90g (3oz) butter
90g (3oz) plain flour
300ml (½ pint) single cream
3 tbsp chopped parsley
1 tbsp chopped fresh dill
salt and black pepper

FISHERMAN'S LASAGNE

1 Put the haddock into a large pan with the onion, bay leaf, peppercorns, and wine. Add enough water to cover, bring to a boil, and simmer for 5 minutes or until the fish is just cooked.

2 Lift out the fish, remove the skin and bones, and flake the flesh. Mix the fish with the prawns. Strain the liquid and make up to 900ml (1½ pints) with water. Set aside.

3 Melt the butter in a saucepan over a medium heat, add the courgettes and garlic, and cook for 3 minutes until beginning to soften.

4 Make the sauce: melt the butter in a saucepan, sprinkle in the flour, and cook, stirring, for 1 minute. Remove the pan from the heat, and gradually blend in the reserved cooking liquid. Bring to a boil, stirring until thickened. Simmer for 2–3 minutes. Stir in the cream, parsley, dill, and salt and pepper to taste.

5 Spoon one-third of the fish mixture into a shallow ovenproof dish, top with one-third of the courgettes, and pour over one-third of the sauce. Arrange half of the lasagne in a single layer. Repeat the layers, finishing with sauce.

6 Sprinkle with the Cheddar and Parmesan cheese and bake in a preheated oven at 200°C (400°F, Gas 6) for 40 minutes or until golden.

SPAGHETTI BOLOGNESE

SERVES 4

3 tbsp olive oil
500g (1lb) raw minced beef
1 large onion, finely chopped
2 celery stalks, sliced
1 tbsp plain flour
2 garlic cloves, crushed
90g (3oz) tomato purée
150ml (¼ pint) beef stock
150ml (¼ pint) red wine
1 × 400g (13oz) can chopped tomatoes
1 tbsp redcurrant jelly
salt and black pepper
400g (1lb) spaghetti
grated Parmesan cheese to serve

1 Heat 2 tbsp of the oil in a saucepan. Add the minced beef, onion, and celery, and cook, stirring, for 5 minutes or until the beef is browned. Add the flour, garlic, and tomato purée, and cook, stirring, for about 1 minute.

2 Pour in the stock and wine. Add the tomatoes and redcurrant jelly, season with salt and pepper, and bring to a boil. Cook, stirring, until the mixture has thickened.

3 Lower the heat, partially cover the pan, and simmer very gently, stirring occasionally, for about 1 hour.

4 Meanwhile, cook the spaghetti in boiling salted water for 8–10 minutes until just tender. Drain.

5 Return the spaghetti to the saucepan, add the remaining oil, and toss gently to coat.

6 Divide the spaghetti among warmed serving plates and ladle some of the sauce on top of each serving. Sprinkle with a little Parmesan cheese and hand the remainder separately.

PAELLA

SERVES 6

3 tbsp olive oil
6 chicken thighs
250g (8oz) smoked bacon,
  rind removed, cut into strips
1 large onion, chopped
1 litre (1¾ pints) chicken stock
250g (8oz) tomatoes, chopped
2 garlic cloves, crushed
a few pinches of saffron threads,
  soaked in a little hot water
500g (1lb) short grain rice
1 red and 1 green pepper, halved,
  seeded, and sliced
125g (4oz) frozen peas
salt and black pepper
500g (1lb) mussels, cleaned (page 45)
125g (4oz) cooked peeled prawns

TO FINISH

12 black olives, pitted
6 large cooked prawns, unpeeled
lemon wedges
2 tbsp chopped parsley

1 Heat the oil in a paella pan or a large, deep frying pan or sauté pan. Add the chicken and cook over a medium heat for 10 minutes until browned all over. Add the bacon and onion and cook for 5 minutes.

2 Stir in the stock, tomatoes, garlic, and the saffron with its soaking liquid, and bring to a boil. Add the rice, red and green peppers, and peas, and season with salt and pepper. Cover and bake in a preheated oven at 180°C (350°F, Gas 4) for 35–40 minutes until the rice is nearly tender and the stock has been absorbed.

3 Meanwhile, put the mussels into a large pan with about 1cm (½in) water. Cover tightly, and cook, shaking the pan occasionally, for 5 minutes or until the shells open. Drain the mussels, and throw away any which have not opened: do not try to force them open.

4 Stir the peeled prawns into the paella, cover, and cook gently on the hob for about 5 minutes. Taste for seasoning. Arrange the mussels around the pan, and the olives, large prawns, and lemon wedges on top. Serve hot, sprinkled with parsley.

Healthy option

If you remove the skin from the chicken before cooking this will considerably reduce the fat content of the paella.

RISOTTO AL VERDE

SERVES 4

15g (½oz) butter
3 garlic cloves, crushed
250g (8oz) risotto rice
1 litre (1¾ pints) hot vegetable stock
175ml (6fl oz) single cream
90g (3oz) blue cheese, crumbled
4 tbsp ready made pesto
90g (3oz) Parmesan cheese, grated
4 tbsp pine nuts, lightly toasted
4 tbsp shredded fresh basil

1 Melt the butter in a large saucepan. When it is foaming, add the garlic and cook gently for 1 minute.

2 Add the risotto rice, stirring to coat the grains in the butter, and cook for 2 minutes. Add a ladleful of the hot vegetable stock, and cook gently, stirring constantly, until the stock has been absorbed. Continue to add the stock, a ladleful at a time, and cook for 20–25 minutes or until the rice is just tender.

3 Add the cream, and cook gently, stirring, until it has been absorbed. Stir in the blue cheese, then the pesto, Parmesan, and pine nuts. Garnish with shredded fresh basil, and serve.

Chicken and mushroom risotto

Add 125g (4oz) sliced mushrooms to the saucepan with the garlic in step 1 and cook for 3–5 minutes until the mushrooms are soft. Substitute chicken stock for the vegetable stock, omit the blue cheese and pesto, then add 250g (8oz) cooked diced chicken with the cream in step 3.

Asparagus risotto

Add 1 finely chopped onion to the pan with the garlic in step 1, and cook for 3–5 minutes until soft. Omit the blue cheese and pesto, and add 375g (12oz) trimmed and chopped asparagus in step 2, about 5 minutes before the end of the cooking time.

Vegetable and Salad Sides

TRICOLORE SALAD

SERVES 4

4 beefsteak or slicing tomatoes
salt and black pepper
250g (8oz) mozzarella cheese
2 avocados
2 tbsp lemon juice
3–4 tbsp extra virgin olive oil
basil sprigs to garnish

1 Slice the tomatoes thinly, put into a bowl, and sprinkle with salt and pepper. Thinly slice the mozzarella.

2 Cut the avocados in half lengthways. Twist to loosen the halves and pull them apart. Remove the stones, score and peel off the skin, then cut the halves crossways.

3 Cut the avocado quarters into thin slices lengthways, then sprinkle with the lemon juice to prevent discoloration.

4 Arrange the tomato, mozzarella, and avocado slices attractively on a platter. Drizzle with the extra virgin olive oil and garnish with basil sprigs before serving.

CREAMED SPINACH

SERVES 4

750g (1½lb) fresh spinach
45g (1½oz) butter
125ml (4fl oz) crème fraîche
¼ tsp grated nutmeg
salt and black pepper
1–2 tbsp grated Parmesan cheese

1 Cut any coarse outer leaves and stalks off the spinach and discard, then wash the spinach thoroughly in plenty of cold water.

2 Melt the butter in a saucepan, add the spinach, and stir until it has absorbed the butter.

3 Add half of the crème fraîche, season with the nutmeg and salt and pepper, and heat through.

4 Transfer to a shallow flameproof dish, pour the remaining crème fraîche on top, and sprinkle with grated Parmesan. Put under a hot grill for a few minutes until lightly browned. Serve hot.

FRENCH-STYLE PEAS

SERVES 4–6

1 small round lettuce, shredded
6 spring onions, chopped
60g (2oz) butter
1 tbsp chopped parsley
1 tsp caster sugar
500g (1lb) shelled fresh peas
  (they must be young)
  or frozen peas
4 tbsp water
salt and black pepper

1 Line the bottom of a saucepan with the lettuce. Add the spring onions, butter, parsley, and sugar, and top with the peas. Add the water, season with salt and pepper, and bring to a boil.

2 Simmer gently, uncovered, for 15–20 minutes until the liquid has evaporated and the peas are tender. Taste for seasoning and serve hot.

GOLDEN ROASTED PUMPKIN

SERVES 6–8

1kg (2lb) piece of pumpkin or butternut
   squash, skinned, seeded, and cut into
   large chunks
2–3 tbsp olive oil
1 tsp balsamic or red wine vinegar
3 garlic cloves, crushed
1 tsp chopped fresh thyme
1 tsp paprika
salt and black pepper
viniagrette dressing (see below)
fresh thyme to garnish

1 Put the pumpkin or buternut squash chunks on a baking tray. Mix the oil, vinegar, garlic, thyme, and paprika, season with salt and pepper, and pour over the pumpkin.

2 Roast in a preheated oven at 190°C (375°F, Gas 5) for 15–20 minutes until the pumpkin is tender and lightly browned on top. Garnish with thyme, and serve at once. If preferred, leave to cool and serve with a vinaigrette dressing.

VINIAGRETTE DRESSING

Put 6 tbsp olive oil, 2 tbsp white wine vinegar, 1 tbsp Dijon mustard, ¼ tsp caster sugar, and a pinch of salt and pepper into a screw-topped jar. Shake well until combined. This makes 150ml (¼ pint).

POMMES ANNA

SERVES 6

750g (1½lb) potatoes
90g (3oz) butter, plus extra for greasing
salt and black pepper

1 Slice the potatoes very thinly, preferably with the slicing disc of a food processor.

2 Generously butter the base and sides of an ovenproof frying pan. Layer the potatoes in the frying pan, seasoning each layer with salt and pepper, and dotting with the butter.

3 Cover the pan tightly with buttered foil and the lid, and cook over a medium heat for 15 minutes or until the base of the potato cake is light golden brown.

4 Transfer the pan to a preheated oven and cook at 190°C (375°F, Gas 5) for 30 minutes or until the potato cake is tender.

5 Invert a warmed serving platter over the pan, and turn out the potato cake so that the crisp layer is on the top. Serve at once, cut into wedges.

Cook's know-how

Arrange the potatoes in the frying pan as soon as they have been sliced. Don't leave them to soak in water or the starch in them will leach out and they will not hold together to make the cake.

COUSCOUS SALAD

SERVES 4–6

½ tsp crushed dried red chillies
90ml (3fl oz) olive oil
250g (8oz) couscous
500ml (16fl oz) boiling water
3–4 tbsp sultanas
5cm (2in) piece of fresh root
  ginger, peeled and grated
salt and black pepper
3–4 tbsp white wine vinegar
5 ripe tomatoes, diced
1 onion, chopped
3 spring onions, thinly sliced
2 tbsp chopped fresh mint
mint sprigs to garnish

1 Combine the chillies and olive oil, and set aside.

2 Put the couscous into a bowl, stir in the measured water, sultanas, ginger, and a good pinch of salt. Cover and leave to stand for 10 minutes.

3 Stir in the chilli oil, vinegar, tomatoes, onion, spring onions, and mint. Season with salt and pepper to taste, and garnish with mint sprigs before serving.

ITALIAN FENNEL

SERVES 8

4 fennel bulbs, trimmed and
quartered lengthways
salt and black pepper
butter for greasing
250g (8oz) mozzarella cheese,
grated chopped parsley to garnish

1 Cook the fennel in boiling salted water for 10 minutes until just tender. Drain thoroughly.

2 Butter a shallow ovenproof dish. Add the fennel and season with salt and pepper. Sprinkle the grated mozzarella cheese on top.

3 Bake in a preheated oven at 200°C (400°F, Gas 6) for 15–20 minutes until the cheese topping is golden and bubbling. Sprinkle with chopped parsley, and serve hot.

CRUNCHY COLESLAW

SERVES 8

1 white cabbage, weighing
  about 750g (1½lb)
150ml (¼ pint) vinaigrette
  dressing (page 205)
1 small onion, finely chopped
1 tsp Dijon mustard
salt and black pepper
3 celery stalks, thinly sliced
2 carrots, grated
60g (2oz) sultanas
75–90ml (2½–3 floz) mayonnaise
  (see below)

1 Cut the cabbage into quarters lengthways and cut out the core. Shred the cabbage finely, using either a sharp knife or the slicing blade of a food processor.

2 Put the cabbage into a large bowl, add the vinaigrette, onion, and Dijon mustard, and season with salt and pepper. Toss to mix thoroughly. Cover the bowl tightly, and leave to chill for about 8 hours.

3 Add the celery, carrots, and sultanas, and toss to mix thoroughly. Stir in the mayonnaise. Cover and chill until ready to serve. Toss the coleslaw well and taste for seasoning before serving.

MAYONNAISE

Put a bowl on a tea towel to steady it. Add 2 egg yolks, 1 tsp Dijon mustard, add salt and pepper to taste, and beat together with a balloon whisk until the egg yolks have thickened slightly. Whisk in 150ml (¼ pint) olive or sunflower oil, or a mixture of the two, just a drop at a time, whisking until the mixture is thick. Stir in 2 tsp white wine vinegar or lemon juice. Check the seasoning, adding sugar to taste if liked. Serve at once or chill. This recipe makes 200ml (7fl oz).

SWISS ROSTI

SERVES 8

1.5kg (3lb) large baking
  potatoes, scrubbed
black pepper
60g (2oz) butter
2 tbsp sunflower oil
fresh thyme to garnish

1 Cook the potatoes in boiling salted water for about 15–20 minutes until just tender. Drain the potatoes thoroughly, leave to cool, then peel. Cover and chill for about 4 hours.

2 Coarsely grate the potatoes into a large bowl, season with pepper, and stir carefully to mix.

3 Melt 30 g (1 oz) of the butter with 1 tbsp of the oil in a frying pan, add the grated potato, and flatten into a cake with a fish slice. Cook over a low heat for about 15 minutes until the base is crisp and golden brown. Turn on to a large buttered plate.

4 Melt the remaining butter and oil in the frying pan, slide in the potato cake, and cook for 5–10 minutes to brown the second side. Turn out on to a warmed platter, garnish, and serve cut into wedges.

Celeriac rosti

Substitute 750g (1½lb) celeriac for half of the potato. Before boiling in step 1, peel the celeriac, and toss in lemon juice to prevent discoloration.

Onion rosti

Heat 1 tbsp sunflower oil in a frying pan, add 1 large chopped onion, and cook for 3–5 minutes until softened but not coloured. Fork the onion into the grated potato in step 2, before seasoning with pepper.

Desserts

Fruit Desserts

CHERRIES JUBILEE

SERVES 4

1 × 425g (14oz) jar or can
  Morello cherries in syrup
2–3 tbsp caster sugar
75 ml (2½fl oz) brandy
a few drops of almond extract
vanilla ice cream to serve

1 Drain the cherries, reserving 125ml (4fl oz) of the syrup. Put the cherries into a saucepan with the measured syrup and the sugar.

2 Heat gently, stirring, until the sugar has dissolved, then bring to a boil. Simmer for about 5 minutes until the liquid has thickened and reduced by about half.

3 Pour the brandy over the cherries, and add the almond extract. Boil to evaporate the alcohol, then spoon the hot cherries and syrup over scoops of vanilla ice cream, and serve at once.

Cook's know-how

Instead of boiling the syrup until it is reduced in step 2, stir in 1 tsp cornflour mixed to a paste with a little cold water. Bring to a boil, stirring, until thickened.

Fresh cherries jubilee

Replace the Morello cherries with 500g (1lb) fresh cherries. Pit the cherries and poach them in 250ml (8fl oz) red wine and 100g (3½oz) caster sugar until tender. Substitute the poaching liquid for the syrup.

MANGO AND LIME MOUSSE

SERVES 6

2 large ripe mangoes
grated zest and juice of 2 limes
15g (½oz) powdered gelatine
3 eggs, plus 1 egg yolk
45g (1½oz) caster sugar
150ml (¼ pint) double or whipping
   cream, whipped until thick

DECORATION

150ml (¼ pint) double or whipping
   cream, whipped until thick
1 lime, thinly sliced

1 Slice the mango flesh away from the stones. Peel the flesh, then purée in a blender or food processor. Add the lime zest to the purée.

2 Put the lime juice into a small bowl, sprinkle the gelatine over the top, and leave for 10 minutes until it becomes spongy.

3 Stand the bowl in a pan of hot water and heat until the gelatine has dissolved.

4 Combine the eggs, egg yolk, and sugar in a large bowl and whisk vigorously for about 10 minutes until the mixture is pale and very thick. Gradually add the mango purée, whisking between each addition to keep the mixture thick.

5 Fold the whipped cream into the mango mixture. Add the dissolved gelatine in a steady stream, stirring gently to mix. Pour the mixture into a glass serving bowl and chill until set.

6 To decorate, pipe rosettes of whipped cream on top of the mousse. Cut the lime slices in half and place between the cream. Serve chilled.

MAGIC LEMON PUDDING

SERVES 4

SHALLOW 600ML (1 PINT) OVENPROOF DISH

60g (2oz) butter, softened,
  plus extra for greasing
grated zest and juice of 1 large lemon
90g (3oz) caster sugar
2 eggs, separated
30g (1oz) plain flour
175ml (6fl oz) milk
lemon or lime slices to decorate

1 Put the butter, lemon zest, and sugar into a bowl and beat together until pale and fluffy.

2 Add the egg yolks, flour, and lemon juice, and stir to combine. Gradually stir in the milk until evenly mixed.

3 Whisk the egg whites until stiff but not dry. Gradually fold into the lemon mixture.

4 Lightly butter the ovenproof dish. Pour the lemon mixture into the dish, and put the dish into a roasting tin. Add enough hot water to the roasting tin to come almost to the rim of the dish. Bake in a preheated oven at 160°C (325°F, Gas 3) for 40 minutes or until the sponge feels springy. Serve hot, decorated with lemon or lime slices. Leftovers are good cold.

Cook's know-how
This "magic" pudding separates during cooking to form a sponge topping with a tangy lemon sauce beneath.

SERVES 4

4 ripe peaches, peeled, stoned, and sliced
8 scoops of vanilla ice cream
mint sprigs to decorate

MELBA SAUCE

375g (12oz) raspberries
about 4 tbsp icing sugar

PEACH MELBA

1 Make the Melba sauce: purée 250g (8oz) of the raspberries. Push through a sieve to remove the seeds. Sift the icing sugar over the purée and stir in.

2 Make an attractive arrangement with the peach slices in 4 glass serving dishes. Top each with 2 scoops of ice cream and some sauce. Decorate with mint sprigs and the remaining raspberries.

FRENCH APRICOT AND ALMOND TART

SERVES 10

28CM (11IN) LOOSE-BOTTOMED FLUTED FLAN TIN
BAKING BEANS

1kg (2lb) fresh apricots,
  halved and stoned
juice of 1 lemon
125ml (4fl oz) water
75g (2½oz) caster sugar
1 tsp arrowroot
crème pâtissière (see below)
1 tbsp brandy
30g (1oz) toasted flaked almonds

PASTRY

250g (8oz) plain flour
125g (4oz) chilled butter, cubed
60g (2oz) caster sugar
1 egg, beaten

CRÉME PÂTISSIÈRE

Put 3 eggs, 90g (3oz) vanilla sugar, and 60g (2oz) plain flour into a large bowl, add a little milk taken from 400ml (14fl oz), and mix until smooth. Pour the remaining milk into a heavy saucepan and bring almost to a boil. Pour on to the egg mixture, whisking well. Rinse out the saucepan to remove any milk residue. Return the egg mixture to the pan, and cook over a gentle heat, stirring continuously, until thickened. Pour into a bowl and cover with cling film, gently pressing it over the surface of the custard to prevent a skin from forming. Leave to cool.

1 Sift the flour into a large bowl. Add the butter and rub in until the mixture resembles fine breadcrumbs. Stir in the sugar and egg to make a soft dough.

2 Roll out the pastry on a lightly floured surface and use to line the flan tin. Chill in the refrigerator for 30 minutes. Bake blind in a preheated oven at 200°C (400°F, Gas 6) for 10 minutes until the pastry case is beginning to brown. Remove the beans and foil and bake for another 5–10 minutes. Leave to cool.

3 Put the apricots, cut-side down, in a shallow pan with the lemon juice, measured water, and sugar. Cover tightly and bring to a boil. Lower the heat and simmer gently for 3 minutes or until just soft. Remove the apricots with a slotted spoon, reserving the juices. Drain on paper towels, and leave to cool.

4 Remove the pastry case from the flan tin and put on a serving plate. Spread the crème pâtissière over the pastry case, and smooth the surface. Arrange the apricots, cut-side down, on the crème pâtissière. Combine the arrowroot and brandy in a small bowl and stir in the reserved apricot juices.

5 Return the mixture to the pan and bring to a boil, stirring until thick. Add the toasted flaked almonds. Spoon the glaze over the apricots, making sure they are evenly coated. (Add a little water to the glaze if it is too thick.) Leave to cool until set and serve cold.

WINTER FRUIT SALAD

SERVES 6

60g (2oz) caster sugar
90ml (3fl oz) water
pared zest of ½ lemon
2 pink grapefruit
2 oranges
250g (8oz) seedless green grapes, halved
2 ripe pears, peeled, cored, and sliced
2 bananas, sliced

1 Put the sugar and measured water into a saucepan and heat gently until the sugar has dissolved. Add the lemon zest and bring the syrup to a boil. Boil for 1 minute, then strain into a serving bowl. Leave to cool.

2 Using a sharp serrated knife, cut the peel and pith from each grapefruit and orange. Remove the segments by cutting between each membrane. Add the segments to the bowl.

3 Add the grapes, pears, and bananas to the serving bowl and gently mix to coat all of the fruit in the sugar syrup.

4 Cover and chill the fruit salad for up to 1 hour before serving.

Cook's know-how

If you are short of time you can just sprinkle the fruit with caster sugar to taste rather than making a sugar syrup. To prevent the pears and bananas from discolouring when sliced and exposed to the air, toss the pieces in lemon juice.

Summer berry salad

Cut 750g (1½lb) strawberries in half, then mix them with 250g (8oz) raspberries and 250g (8oz) blueberries. Sift 3 tbsp icing sugar over the fruit, and pour the juice of 2 oranges on top. Stir gently, cover, and chill for 1 hour.

MANGO AND PASSION FRUIT MERINGUE

SERVES 6

4 egg whites
250g (8oz) caster sugar

FILLING

1 ripe mango
1 passion fruit
300ml (½ pint) whipping cream,
  whipped until thick
125g (4oz) strawberries, sliced

DECORATION

150ml (¼ pint) double or whipping
  cream, whipped until stiff
a few strawberries

1 Mark 2 × 20cm (8in) circles on 2 sheets of non-stick baking parchment, turn the paper over, and use to line 2 baking trays.

2 Whisk the egg whites with a hand-held electric mixer until stiff but not dry. Add the sugar, 1 tsp at a time, and continue to whisk until all the sugar has been incorporated and the mixture is stiff and glossy.

3 Pipe the meringue, in concentric circles, inside the marked circles on the paper-lined baking trays.

4 Bake the meringue rounds in a preheated oven at 140°C (275°F, Gas 1) for 1–1¼ hours until crisp and dry. Leave to cool, then carefully peel off the paper.

5 Dice the mango very fine. Halve the passion fruit and scoop out the pulp.

6 Spread the whipped cream over 1 of the meringue rounds. Arrange the mango, passion fruit pulp, and strawberries on top, and cover with the remaining meringue round.

7 Decorate with piped rosettes of whipped cream, strawberry slices, and a whole strawberry.

PLUM CRUMBLE

SERVES 6

1kg (2lb) plums, halved and stoned
60g (2oz) light muscovado sugar
1 tsp ground cinnamon

CRUMBLE TOPPING

250g (8oz) self-raising brown flour
100g (4oz) butter
150g (5oz) light muscovado sugar

1 Put the plums into a shallow ovenproof dish and sprinkle with the sugar and cinnamon.

2 Make the topping: put the flour into a bowl, and rub in the butter with the fingertips until the mixture resembles fine breadcrumbs. Stir in the sugar.

3 Sprinkle the topping evenly over the plums, without pressing it down, and bake in a preheated oven at 180°C (350°F, Gas 4) for 30–40 minutes until golden. Serve the crumble hot with custard.

Crunchy apricot crumble

Substitute fresh apricots for the plums, and omit the cinnamon. Substitute porridge oats or muesli for half of the flour in the crumble topping, or use up to 125g (4oz) chopped toasted hazelnuts. You can also use half white and half brown flour.

Rhubarb and ginger crumble

Substitute 1kg (2lb) rhubarb, cut into 2.5cm (1in) pieces, for the plums. Put into a saucepan with the sugar, 2 tbsp water, and 1 tsp ground ginger instead of the cinnamon, and cook gently until the rhubarb is soft.

Rich Desserts

SCOTCH MIST

SERVES 6

450ml (¾ pint) double or
  whipping cream
4 tbsp whisky
90g (3oz) meringues, coarsely crushed
30g (1oz) flaked almonds, toasted

1 Whip the cream with the whisky until it just holds its shape. Fold in the crushed meringues.

2 Spoon the mixture into 6 glass serving bowls, cover, and chill for about 20 minutes or until firm.

3 Scatter the toasted flaked almonds over the desserts just before serving.

Eton mess

Substitute 4 tbsp brandy for the whisky, and add 500g (1lb) chopped strawberries to the cream mixture. Decorate with strawberry halves and mint leaves instead of the almonds.

SERVES 4

4 × 300ML (½ PINT) SOUFFLÉ DISHES

125g (4oz) plain chocolate
2 tbsp water
300ml (½ pint) milk
45g (1½oz) butter, plus extra for greasing
45g (1½oz) plain flour
2–3 drops of vanilla essence
60g (2oz) caster sugar
4 egg yolks
5 egg whites
sifted icing sugar for dusting

HOT CHOCOLATE SOUFFLÉS

1 Break the chocolate into pieces, and put into a small saucepan with the meaured water and a few tablespoons of the milk. Heat gently, stirring, until the chocolate has melted. Add the remaining milk, stirring to blend.

2 Melt the butter in a pan, add the flour, and cook, stirring, for 1 minute. Remove from the heat, and gradually add the chocolate and milk mixture. Bring to a boil, stirring, until the sauce has thickened. Stir in the vanilla essence and caster sugar, and cool.

3 Beat the egg yolks into the cooled chocolate mixture. Lightly butter the individual soufflé dishes and set aside.

4 Whisk the egg whites until stiff but not dry. Stir 1 large spoonful of the egg whites into the chocolate mixture, then carefully fold in the remainder. Divide the mixture between the 4 soufflé dishes.

5 Place on a hot baking tray and bake in a preheated oven at 190°C (375°F, Gas 5) for 40–45 minutes until the soufflés are well risen and firm. Dust with sifted icing sugar. Serve the soufflés at once.

FLOATING ISLANDS

SERVES 4

butter for greasing
3 eggs, separated
205g (7oz) caster sugar
1 tsp vanilla extract
1 tsp cornflour
600ml (1 pint) milk
30g (1oz) flaked almonds, toasted

1 Butter 4 individual serving dishes. Line a baking tray with a sheet of baking parchment.

2 In a large bowl, mix together the egg yolks, 30g (1oz) of the sugar, vanilla extract, and cornflour. In a heavy saucepan, bring the milk to a boil. Add the boiling milk to the egg-yolk mixture, stirring constantly, then pour the mixture back into the pan.

3 Return to the heat and cook gently, stirring constantly, until the froth disappears and the custard is thickened. Pour the custard into the buttered dishes, and leave to cool.

4 Whisk the egg whites until stiff but not dry. Add the rest of the sugar, 1 tsp at a time, and continue to whisk until all the sugar has been incorporated and the mixture is stiff and glossy.

5 Shape the meringue into 8 ovals by scooping it up between 2 tablespoons, and place on the baking tray.

6 Cook in a preheated oven at 160°C (325°F, Gas 3) for 20 minutes until the meringues are set and no longer sticky. Leave to cool, then arrange on top of the custard. Sprinkle with almonds before serving.

POTS AU CHOCOLAT

SERVES 6

175g (6oz) plain dark chocolate,
broken into pieces
3 tbsp strong black coffee
15g (½oz) butter
a few drops of vanilla extract
3 eggs, separated
150ml (¼ pint) double cream,
whipped until stiff, to decorate

1 Put the chocolate pieces into a saucepan with the strong black coffee. Heat gently, stirring, until the chocolate melts.

2 Leave the chocolate mixture to cool slightly, then add the butter, vanilla essence, and egg yolks and stir until well blended.

3 Whisk the egg whites until stiff but not dry. Fold gently but thoroughly into the chocolate mixture.

4 Pour the mixture into 6 small custard pots, ramekins, or other serving dishes, and leave to chill for about 8 hours.

5 Decorate each pot of chocolate with a piped rosette of whipped cream before serving.

SERVES 4–6

6 eggs, separated
175g (6oz) caster sugar
2 tsp vanilla extract
450ml (¾ pint) double cream,
  whipped until thick

QUICK VANILLA ICE CREAM

1 Whisk the egg whites (at high speed if using an electric mixer) until stiff but not dry. Add the sugar, 1 tsp at a time, and continue whisking until the sugar has been incorporated and the egg-white mixture is very stiff and glossy.

2 Put the egg yolks into a separate bowl and whisk at high speed with an electric mixer until the mixture is blended thoroughly.

3 Gently fold the whipped cream, egg yolks, and vanilla extract into the egg-white mixture. Turn into a large shallow freezerproof container, cover, and leave the mixture to freeze for 8 hours.

4 Transfer the ice cream to the refrigerator for about 10 minutes before serving so that it softens slightly.

Lemon ice cream

Omit the vanilla extract. Add the grated zest and juice of 3 large lemons when folding the mixtures in step 3.

Cook's know-how

Pregnant women, babies and young children, and the elderly should avoid eating raw eggs.

CHOCOLATE CHIP CHEESECAKE

SERVES 8

20CM (8IN) LOOSE-BOTTOMED OR SPRINGFORM CAKE TIN

125g (4oz) plain dark chocolate,
 broken into pieces
3 tbsp cold water
15g (½oz) powdered gelatine
250g (8oz) full-fat soft cheese
2 eggs, separated
60g (2oz) caster sugar
150ml (¼ pint) soured cream
30g (1oz) plain dark chocolate
 chips, coarsely chopped

BASE

125g (4oz) muesli
90g (3oz) butter, melted
30g (1oz) demerara sugar

DECORATION

300ml (½ pint) whipping cream,
 whipped until stiff
chocolate curls or caraque

1 Make the base: mix together the muesli, melted butter, and sugar, and press evenly over the bottom of the tin. Chill.

2 Meanwhile, put the chocolate into a small heatproof bowl over a pan of hot, gently simmering, water. Heat gently to melt the chocolate, stirring occasionally. Leave to cool.

3 Put the measured water into a heatproof bowl and sprinkle the gelatine over the top. Leave for 10 minutes until spongy. Stand the bowl in a pan of hot water and heat gently until the gelatine has dissolved.

4 Beat the cheese until smooth. Add the egg yolks and sugar and beat until blended. Stir in the soured cream, melted chocolate, chocolate chips, and gelatine. Mix well.

5 In a separate bowl, whisk the egg whites until stiff but not dry. Fold carefully into the chocolate mixture until evenly mixed. Pour on to the muesli base and chill until set.

6 Use a knife to loosen the side of the cheesecake from the tin, then remove the cheesecake. Slide on to a serving plate. Pipe rosettes of whipped cream on top and decorate with chocolate curls or caraque.

BRANDY SNAPS

MAKES 15

90g (3oz) butter
90g (3oz) demerara sugar
90g (3oz) golden syrup
90g (3oz) plain flour
¾ tsp ground ginger
¾ tsp lemon juice

1 Line a baking tray with baking parchment.

2 Combine the butter, sugar, and syrup in a saucepan and heat gently until the ingredients have melted and dissolved. Cool slightly, then sift in the flour and ginger. Add the lemon juice and stir well.

3 Place 3–4 teaspoonfuls of the mixture on the baking tray, leaving plenty of room for the biscuits to spread out.

4 Bake in a preheated oven at 160°C (325°F, Gas 3) for 8 minutes until the mixture spreads out to form large, thin, dark golden rounds. While the biscuits are baking, oil the handles of 4 wooden spoons.

5 Remove the biscuits from the oven and leave for 1–2 minutes to firm slightly.

6 Lift a biscuit from the paper using a fish slice or palette knife, turn the biscuit over so that the rough side is on the outside, and wrap around an oiled wooden spoon handle. Repeat with the remaining biscuits. Transfer to a wire rack and cool until firm. Slip from the spoon handles.

7 Continue baking, shaping, and cooling the remaining mixture in batches.

INDEX

MARY BERRY

ABOUT THE AUTHOR

Mary Berry is one of the UK's best known and respected cookery writers, a TV cook and Aga expert, and champion of traditional family cooking. With over 60 books to her name, and over 5 million sales worldwide, in 2004 she was voted Top 3 by BBC Good Food for the category "Most Reliable Celebrity Cook Books", alongside Jamie Oliver and Delia Smith.

ACKNOWLEDGMENTS

AUTHOR'S ACKNOWLEDGMENTS FOR *MARY BERRY'S COMPLETE COOKBOOK*

For the first edition, I would like to thank Fiona Oyston for her expertise in writing and testing recipes, and for all her hard work helping me produce the book. I would also like to thank managing editor Gillian Roberts for help in preparing the second edition.

PUBLISHER'S ACKNOWLEDGMENTS FOR *MARY BERRY'S COMPLETE COOKBOOK*

The first (1995) edition of this book was created by Carroll & Brown Ltd for Dorling Kindersley. Thanks to the following people for their help: Editorial consultant, Jeni Wright; Project editor, Vicky Hanson; Editors, Jo-Anne Cox, Stella Vayne, Anne Crane, Sophie Lankenau, and Trish Shine; Cookery consultants, Valerie Cipollone and Anne Hildyard; Art editors, Louise Cameron and Gary Edgar-Hyde; Designers, Alan Watt, Karen Sawyer, and Lucy De Rosa; Photography, David Murray and Jules Selmes, assisted by Nick Allen and Sid Sideris; Production, Wendy Rogers and Amanda Mackie; Food preparation, Eric Treuille, Annie Nichols, Cara Hobday, Sandra Baddeley, and Elaine Ngan, assisted by Maddalena Bastianelli and Sarah Lowman; Additional recipes/Contributors, Marlena Spieler, Sue Ashworth, Louise Pickford, Cara Hobday, Norma MacMillan, and Anne Gains; Nutritional consultant Anne Sheasby.

The second (2003) edition of this book was created by Dorling Kindersley. Thanks to the following people for their help: Editorial contributor, Norma MacMillan; Editorial assistance, Hugh Thompson; DK Picture Library, Claire Bowers and Charlotte Oster; Nutritional consultant, Wendy Doyle; Index, Helen Smith; Loan of props, Villeroy & Boch, Thomas Goode & Co. and Chomett. Thanks also to DK India: Project editor, Dipali Singh; Editor, Kajori Aikat; Project designer, Romi Chakraborty; Designer, Rashmi Battoo; DTP, Narender Kumar, Rajesh Chibber, and Nain Singh Rawat; Managing editor, Ira Pande; Managing art editor, Aparna Sharma.

The publisher would like to thank Susan Bosanko for creating the index and Romaine Werblow for her picture research for *Mary Berry's Supper for Friends*.

The publisher would like to thank the following for their kind permission to reproduce their photographs:

(Key: a-above; b-below/bottom; c-centre; l-left; r-right; t-top)

Jacket images: *Front:* **Rob Judges** and **William Reavell:** tr. *Spine:* **Rob Judges:** t

All other images © Dorling Kindersley
For further information see: www.dkimages.com